CREATIVE ORIGAMI

Written by Irmgard Kneißler

MAGNA BOOKS

By Irmgard Kneißler

Copyright © 1987 by Ravensburger
Buchverlag Otto Maier GmbH
First published in Germany under the titles:
ORIGAMI—PAPIERFALTEN and KREATIVES ORIGAMI
Copyright © 1991 Ottenheimer Publishers, Inc.
All Rights Reserved

This 1991 edition is published by
Ottenheimer Publishers, Inc. for Magna Books,
Magna Road, Wigston, Leicester,
LE8 2ZH, England

Printed and bound in Singapore

ISBN 1 85422 183 3

Table of Contents

INTRODUCTION

Origami is the traditional Japanese art of paper folding. Over the years, origami artists have found more and more intricate ways of folding paper, and origami has become popular all over the world. You, too, can learn the art of paper folding by following the illustrations in this book.

The only material needed for origami is paper. The paper should be thin, hold a crease, and not tear easily when folded a number of times. Special origami paper, which is colored on one side and white on the other, is available at craft and art supply stores. Occasionally scissors are used to cut the folded paper. A piece of wood can be used to create a better fold. Glue is not needed, except to decorate the origami or to glue it onto a box or piece of paper. The Japanese traditionally do not glue eyes onto their models.

FOLDING HINTS

1. Always fold the paper on a hard, flat surface.
2. Make folds as straight and precise as possible, so that corners and edges meet evenly.
3. Crease folds firmly with your thumb or a piece of wood.
4. After each fold, check what you've done by positioning the paper in the same direction as in the diagram.
5. Before making a fold, look ahead to the next fold so you can better understand what you need to do.

TERMS USED IN THIS BOOK

VALLEY FOLD:
The paper is folded downward, or toward you. When you unfold the paper, the crease is on the bottom, looking like a valley.

MOUNTAIN FOLD:
The paper is folded backwards, or away from you. When you unfold the paper, the crease is on top, causing the paper to look like a mountain.

THE CREASE:
The line left when you fold the paper, then unfold it.

TOP:
The corner or edge of the paper that is pointed away from your body.

BOTTOM:
The corner or edge of the paper that is pointed toward your body.

FRONT:
The side of the paper that is facing you as you work.

BACK:
The side of the paper that is facing the table. Circled letters in the diagrams indicate corners or edges that are lying in the back of the model.

RIGHT:
Parts that are lying to the right of the middle line.

OUTSIDE:
The back and front of your work.

INSIDE:
Everything that is between the front and back layers of paper. The letters identifying the corners and edges facing the inside of the model are circled.

UNFOLD:
The last fold is opened up again.

TURNING:
Keeping your work flat on the table, turn the paper so that the corners are aligned as shown in the diagram.

TURNING THE MODEL OVER:
Turn the paper over, so that the front now becomes the back.

OUTSIDE REVERSE FOLD:
The front and back layers of paper are spread apart and wrapped around the outside of the model. The edges that were a valley fold have now become a mountain fold.

INSIDE REVERSE FOLD:
An edge, which is a mountain fold, is pushed down between the front and back layers of the paper. The edge has now become a valley fold.

EXPLANATION OF DIAGRAMS

The following are used in the diagrams in this book:

A **dash line** indicates either a valley fold or an outside reverse fold. Check the text to see which fold is required.

A **dotted line** indicates either a mountain fold or an inside reverse fold. Check the text to see which fold is required.

A **combination dotted** and **striped line** indicates a sharp crease.

A **circled letter** indicates that the tip or corner is facing the inside or back of the model.

THE BASIC FORMS

To make the models in this book, you must first start with one of the following basic forms.

BASIC FORM A

1. Place paper with coloured side face down. Valley fold A-C along dash line. Unfold. Valley fold first A-D, then A-B along crease you just made.

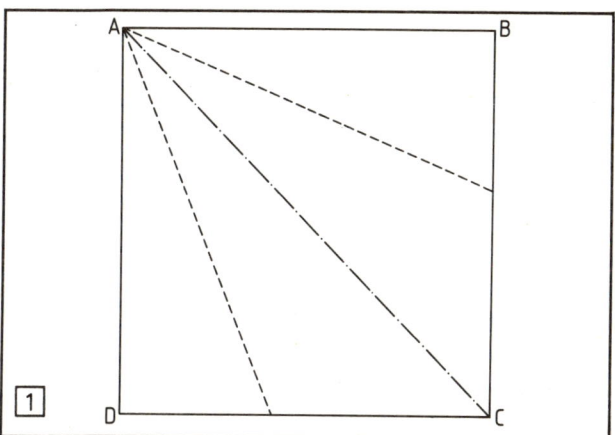

BASIC FORM B

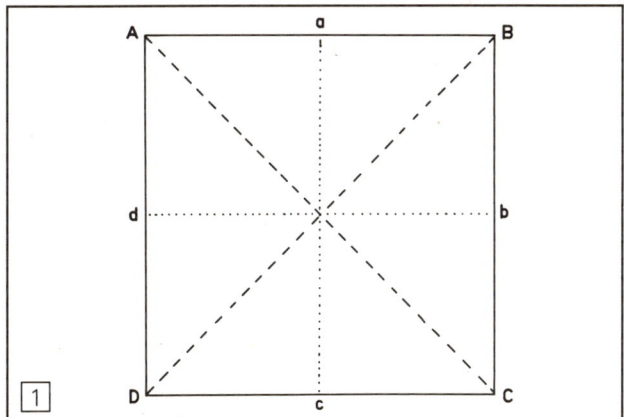

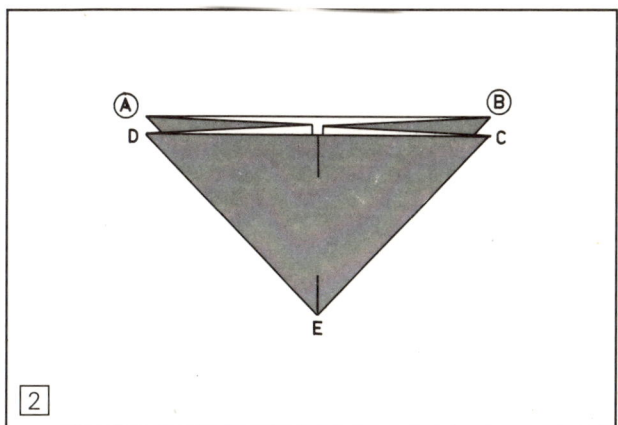

1. Valley fold A-C along dash line. Unfold, then valley fold B-D along dash line. Unfold, then mountain fold along dotted line a-c. Unfold and mountain fold along dotted line d-b. Push points d and b in toward middle and fold model so D is on top of A, and C is on top of B.

2. The finished form.

BASIC FORM C

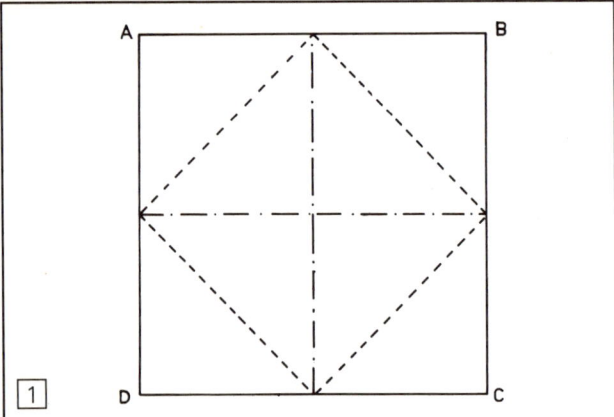

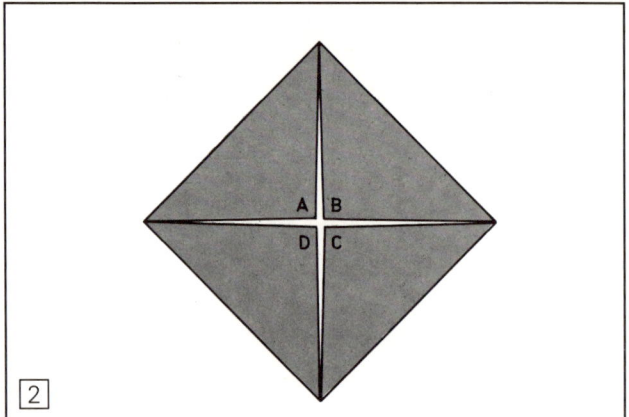

1. Fold paper in half horizontally. Unfold, then fold in half vertically. Unfold. Fold all 4 corners in to middle point.

2. The finished form.

BASIC FORM D

1. Mountain fold along dotted line A-C. Unfold, then mountain fold along dotted line D-B. Unfold and valley fold along one dash line. Unfold, then valley fold along second dash line. With your thumbs, push B and D in to rest on top of A. Fold C on top of A, B, and D.

2. The finished form.

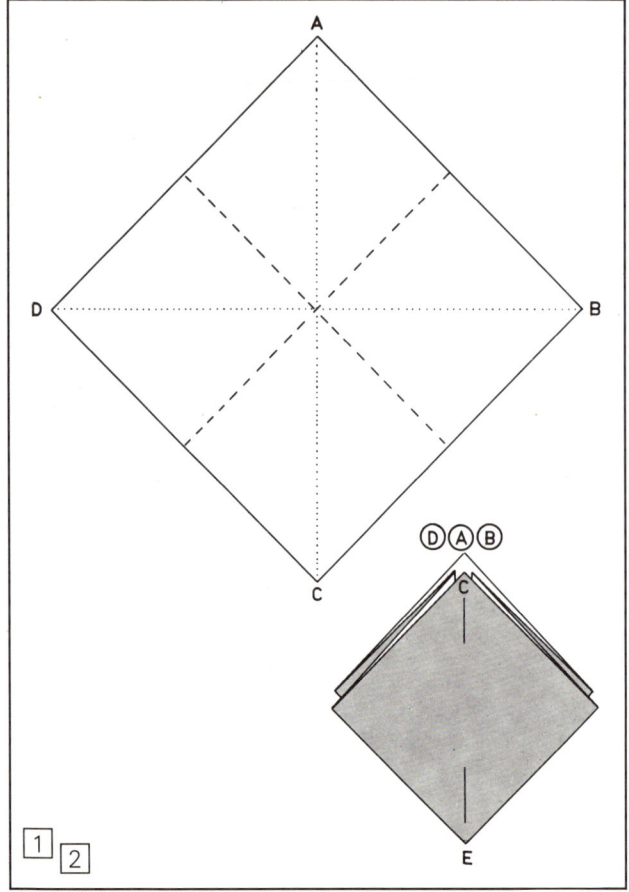

14

BASIC FORM E

1. Start with basic form D. Turn so A is on bottom. Along lines 1, fold F and G to middle line. Unfold. Along line 2, fold E over. Unfold.

2. Pull C in crease made by folding E down. At the same time, push G and F onto middle line and crease well.

3. Turn model over and follow steps 1 and 2 on back side. Turn model over again.

4. The finished form.

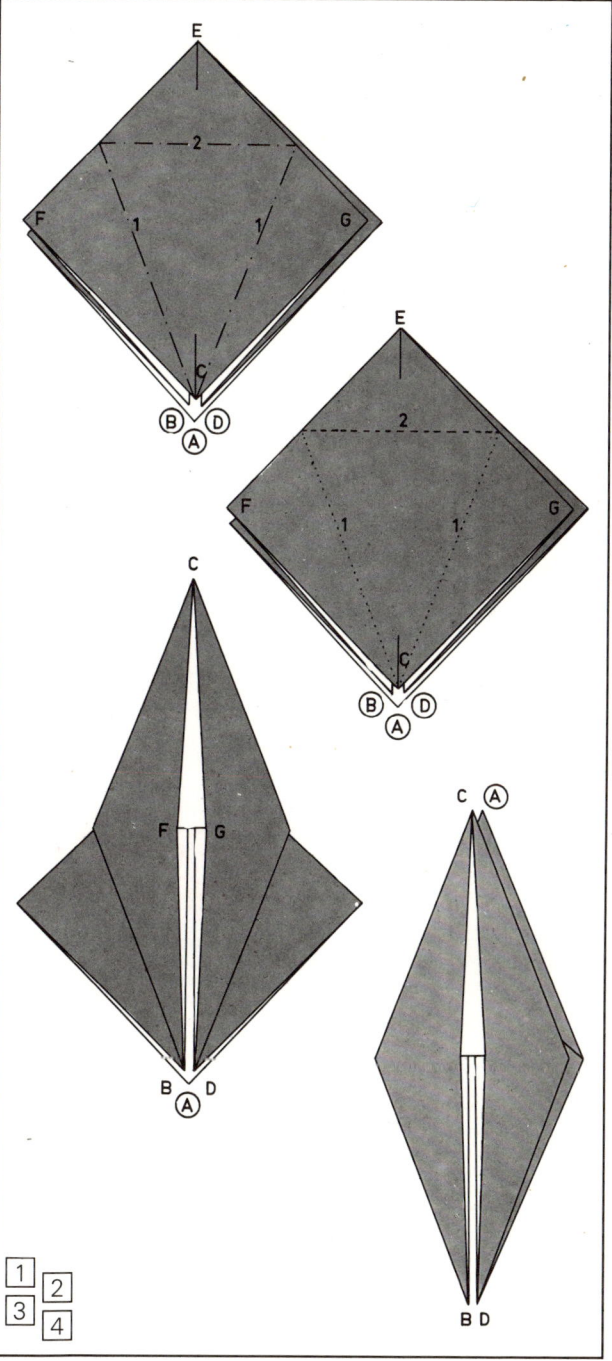

SWAN

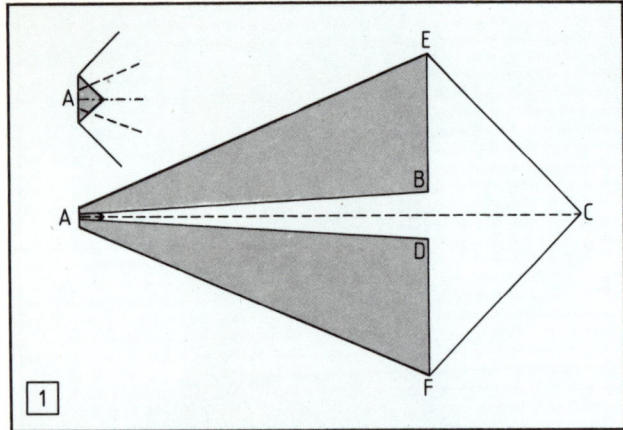

1. Start with Basic Form A. Arrange paper as in diagram. Unfold paper and make a small fold with A (see inset). Refold flaps E-B and D-F over tip A. Fold along centre crease, bringing E to F.

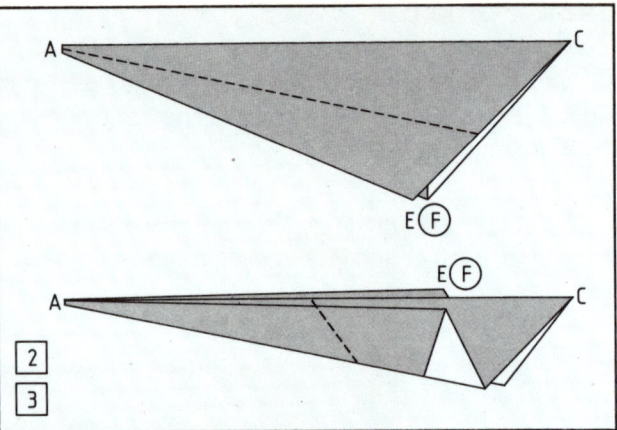

2. Fold A-E up to A-C. Turn model over and fold A-F up to A-C.
3. Outside reverse fold across dash line.

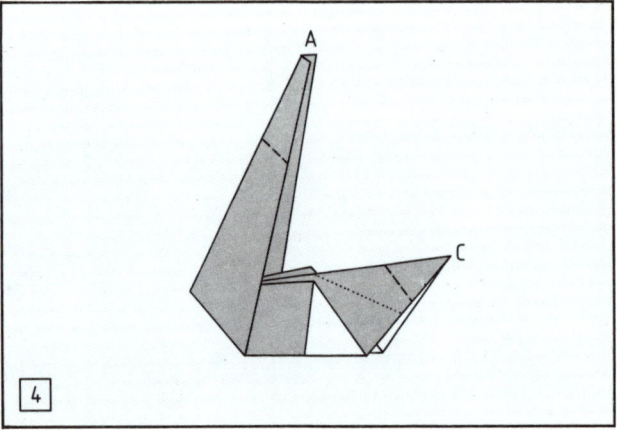

4. Inside reverse fold C down along dotted line. Valley fold C up along dash line, so tail is pointing up. Push in with thumb and crease firmly. Outside reverse fold A to form head.

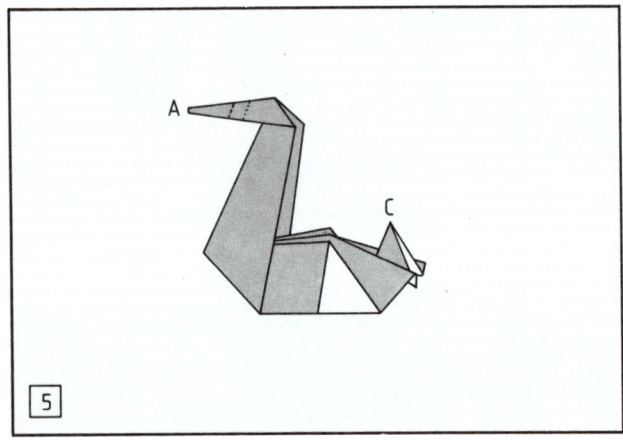

5. Fold in and out along dotted lines to form beak.

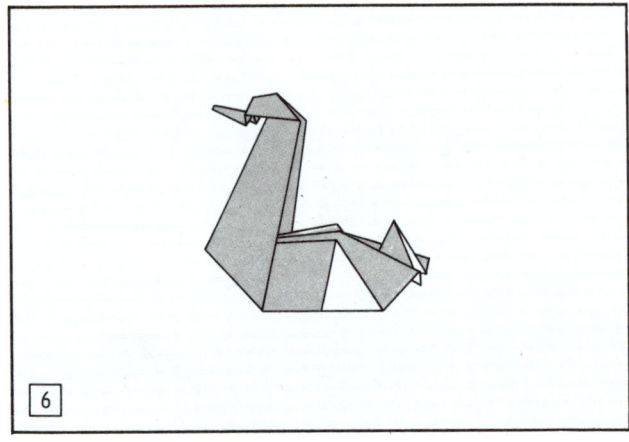

6. The finished swan.

CHICKS & BUNNIES

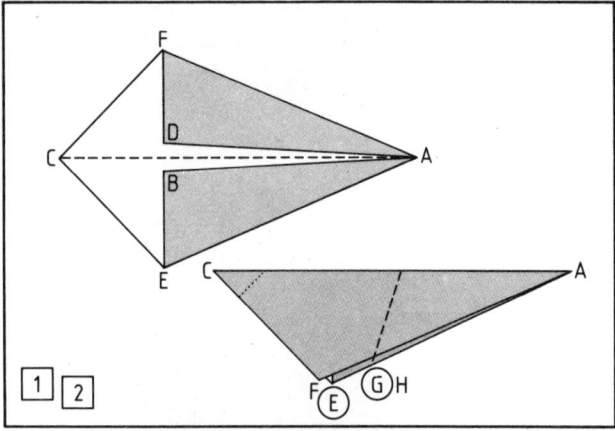

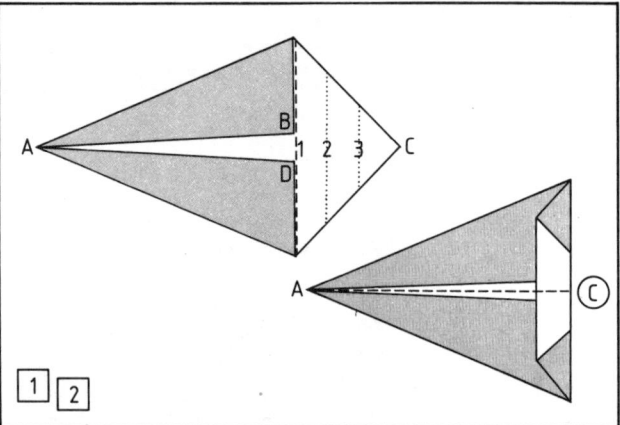

CHICK 1. Start with Basic Form A. Fold along middle crease. 2. Outside reverse fold along dash line to form tail. Inside reverse fold C to make beak.

BUNNY 1. Start with Basic Form A. Valley fold C on dash line. Fold C back on line 2. Fold tip C back on line 3 so C is now on back side of model.
2. Valley fold along middle crease.

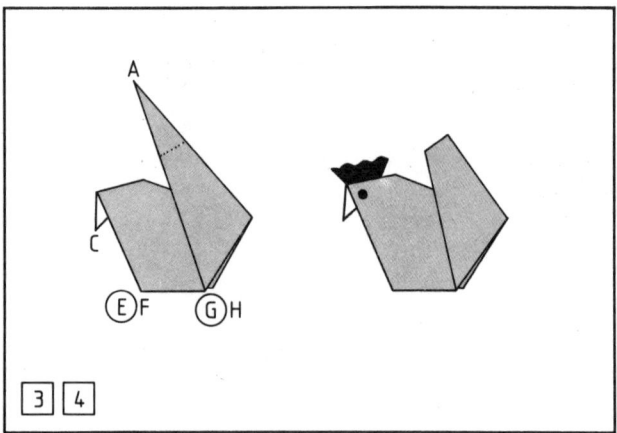

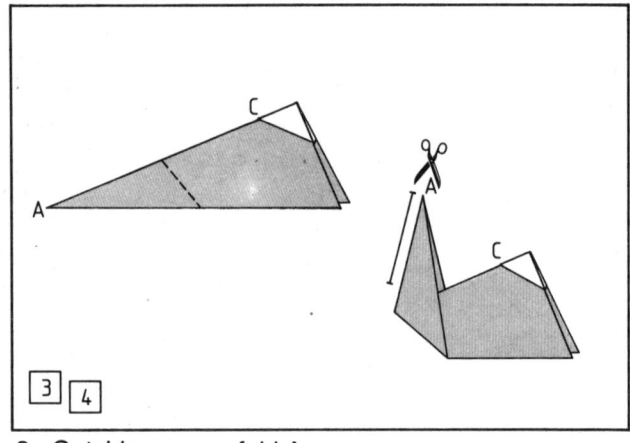

3. Fold A down.
4. Cut comb out of paper and glue on.

3. Outside reverse fold A.
4. Cut out ears on A.

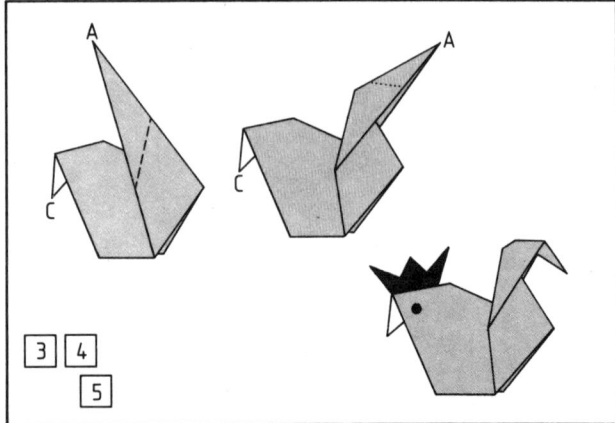

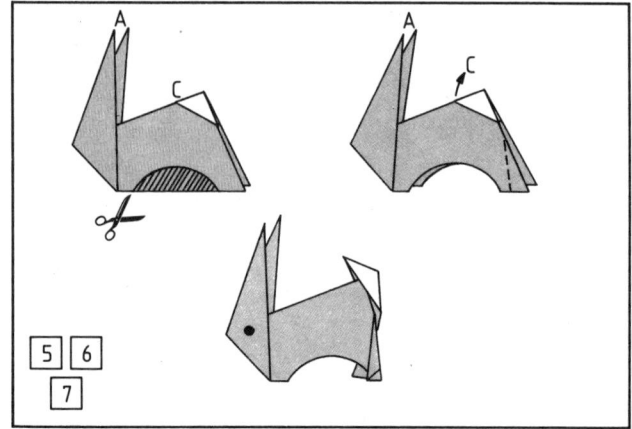

5. To make a rooster, start with diagram 3. Outside reverse fold A. Inside reverse fold A. Cut comb out of paper and glue on.

5. Cut out semicircle on bottom of rabbit.
6. Lightly pull out C. Valley fold along dash line on both sides of model to form back legs.
7. The finished rabbit.

CORMORANT

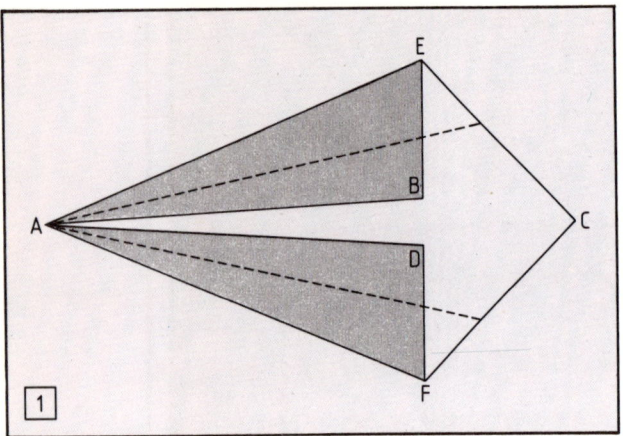

1. Start with Basic Form A. Fold lines A-E and A-F along middle crease.

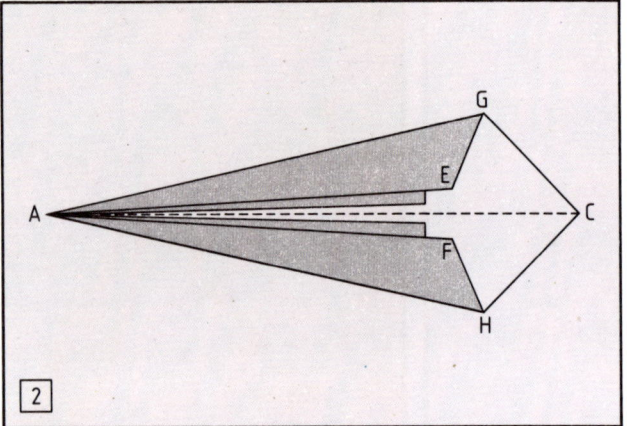

2. Valley fold along dash line.

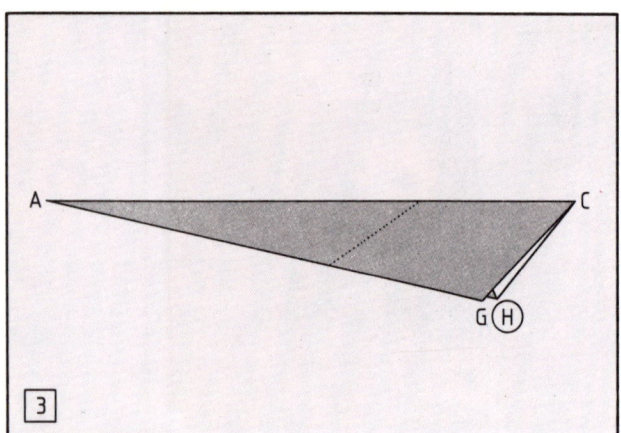

3. Inside reverse fold along dotted line.

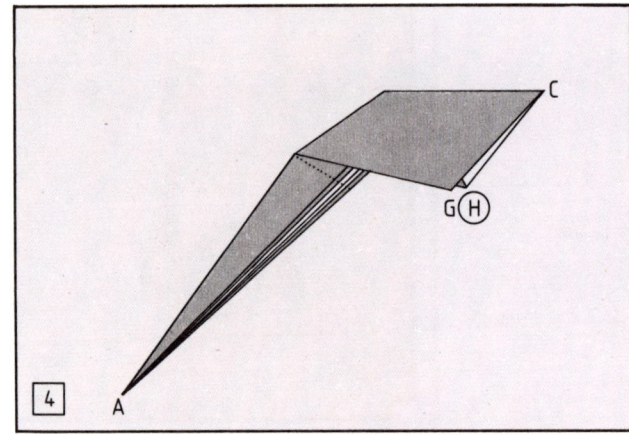

4. This is how your model should now look.

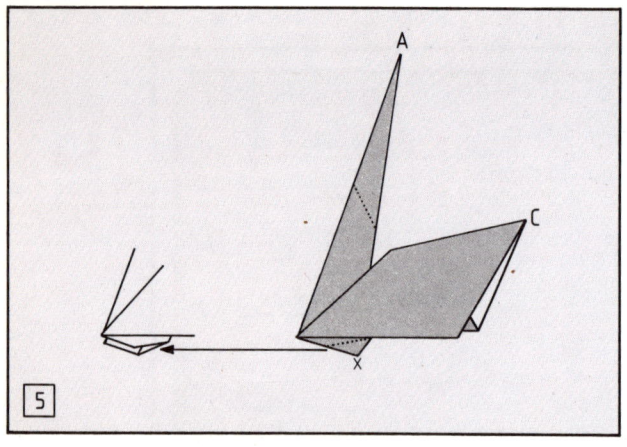

5. Inside reverse fold A along dotted line. Fold x inside model.

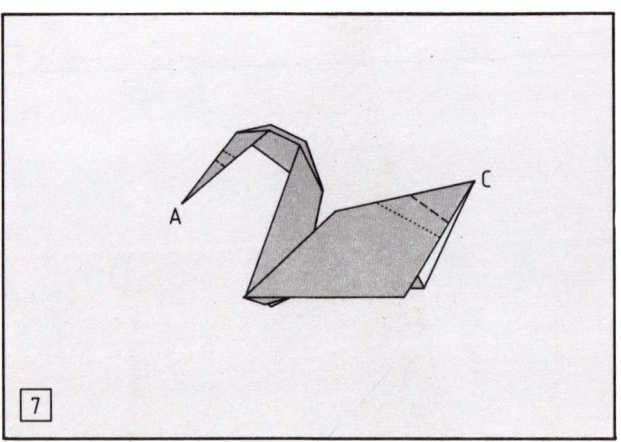

6. Outside reverse fold A along dash line.

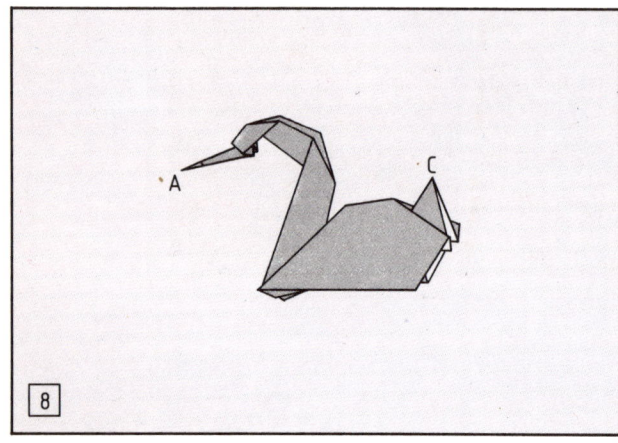

7. Fold back and forward to form beak. Inside reverse fold, then outside reverse fold C to form tail.

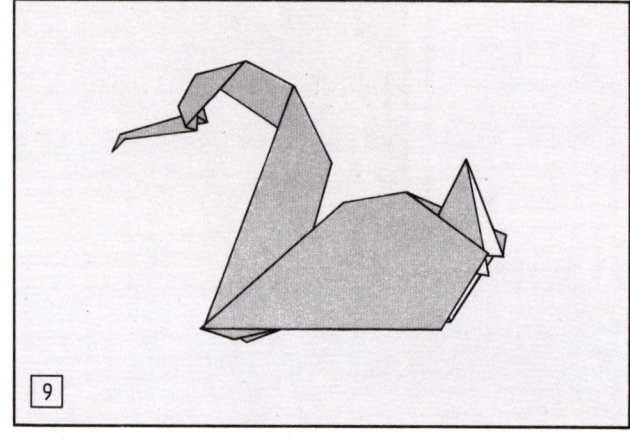

8. Bend tip of beak down.

9. The enlarged, finished model.

ELEPHANT

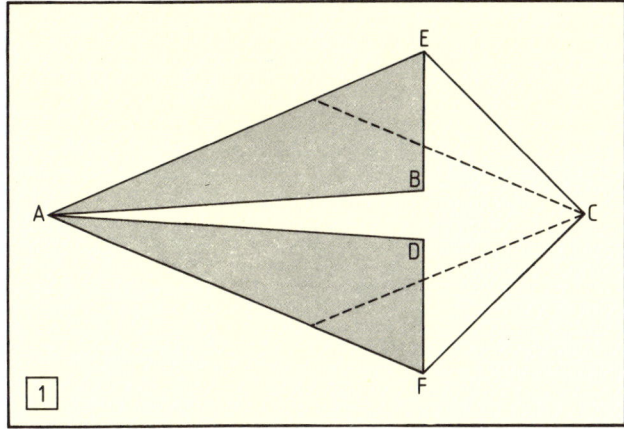

1. Start with Basic Form A. Valley fold C along dash lines.

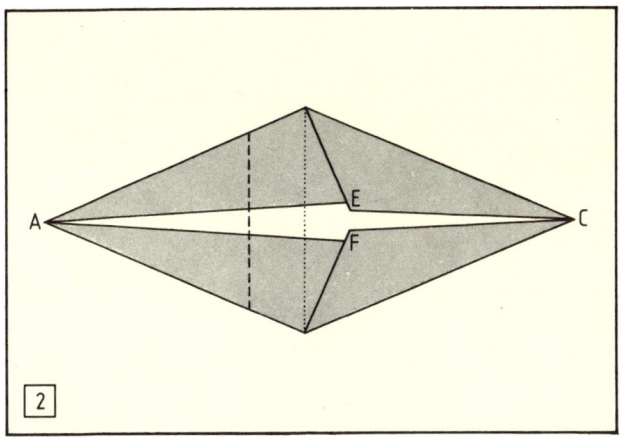

2. Mountain fold A along dotted line, then valley fold along dash line.

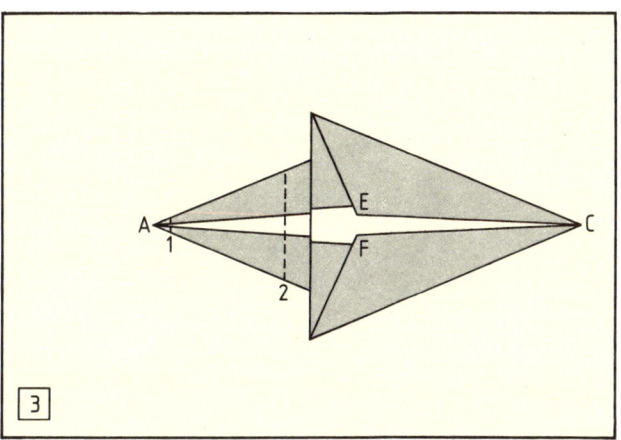

3. Valley fold A along dash line 1, then along dash line 2.

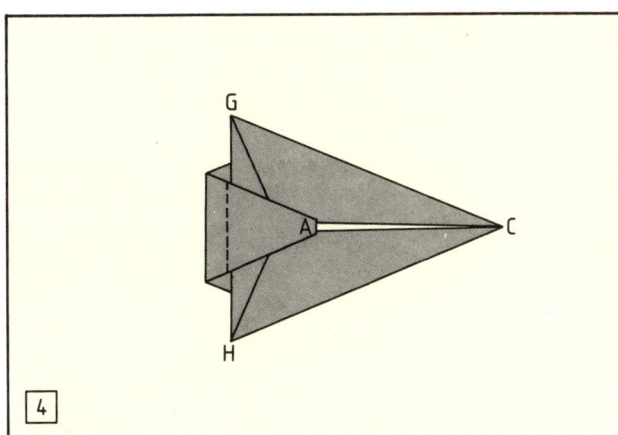

4. Valley fold A back along dash line.

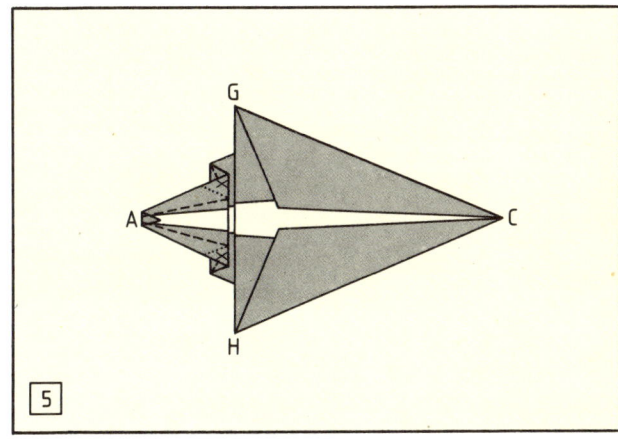

5. Valley fold A along dash line. Mountain fold along dotted lines, forming small triangular cups at points x, as shown in diagram 6.

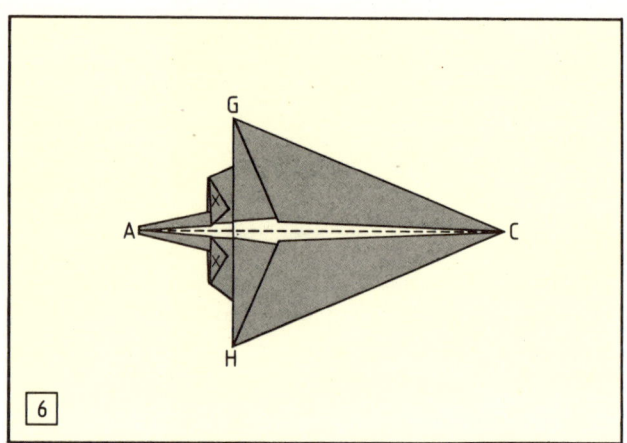

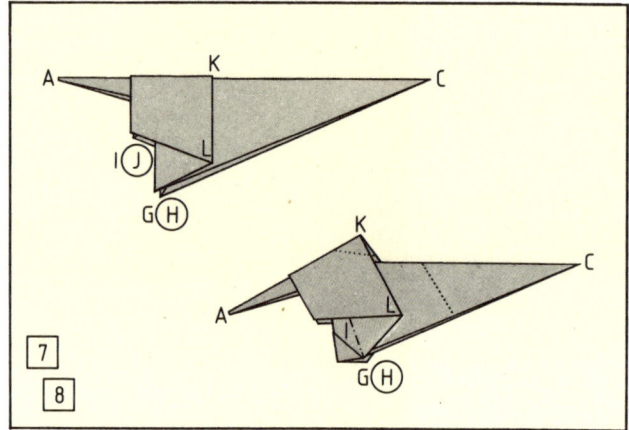

6. Valley fold along middle crease. G goes on H.

7. Your model should now look like this.
8. Pull K up and crease again so K is pointing up as in diagram 8. Inside reverse fold K along dotted line.

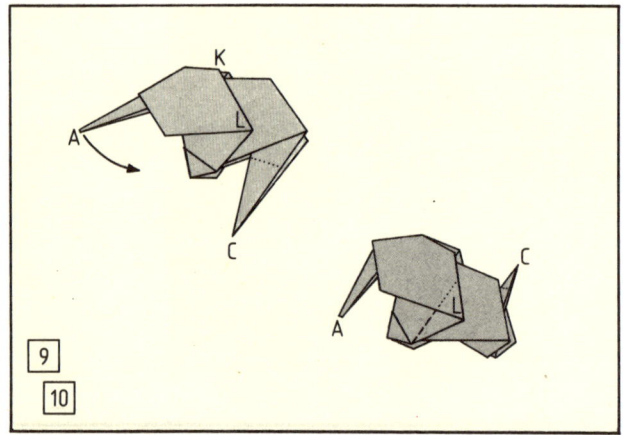

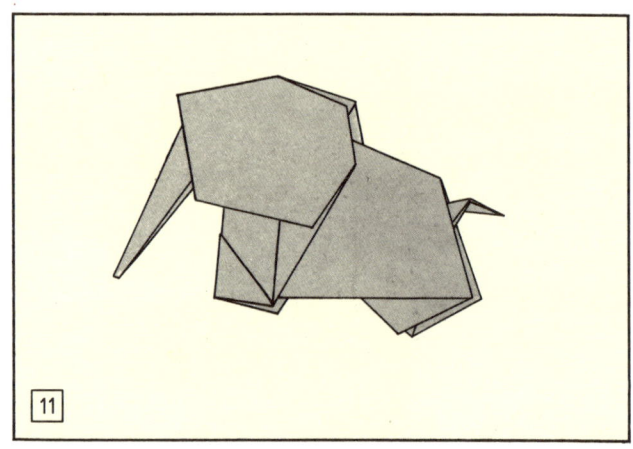

9. Inside reverse fold C along dotted line. A, the trunk, can be placed at any position.
10. Mountain fold L on front and back of model so corners are tucked under ears. Fold C to form tail.

11. The enlarged finished elephant.

RABBIT

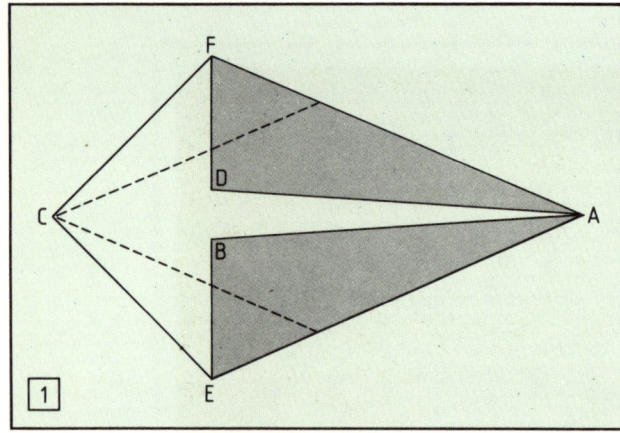

1. Start with Basic Form A. Valley fold C along dash lines.

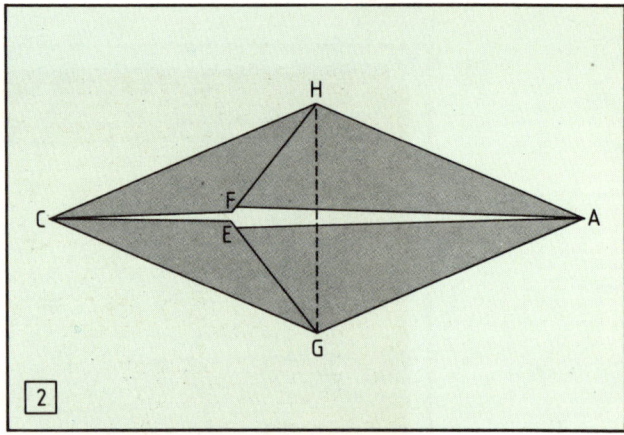

2. Valley fold along dash line. Unfold. Pull out inside corners B and D (see diagram 3) and crease along new fold you just made.

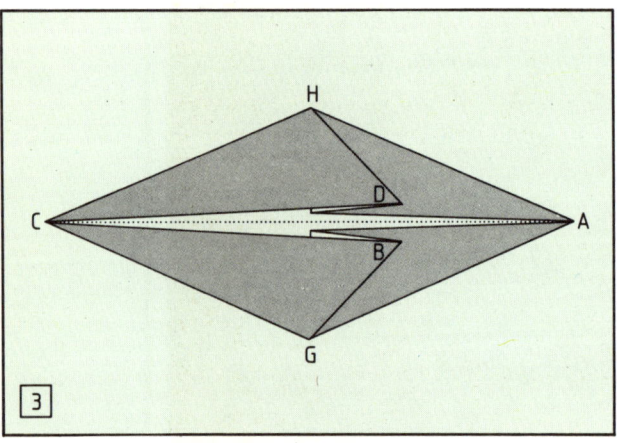

3. Mountain fold along middle crease.

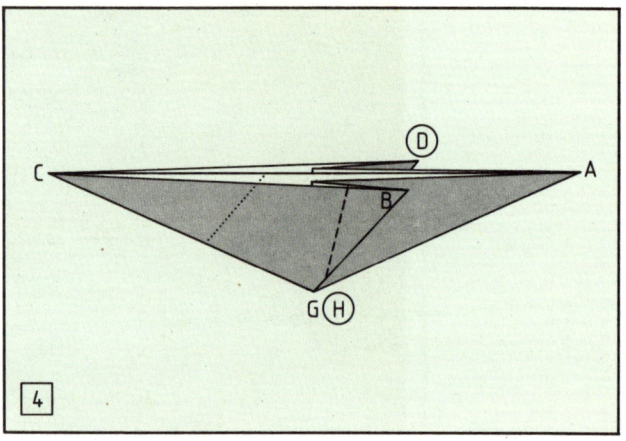

4. Valley fold B and D to form ears. Inside reverse fold C along dotted line.

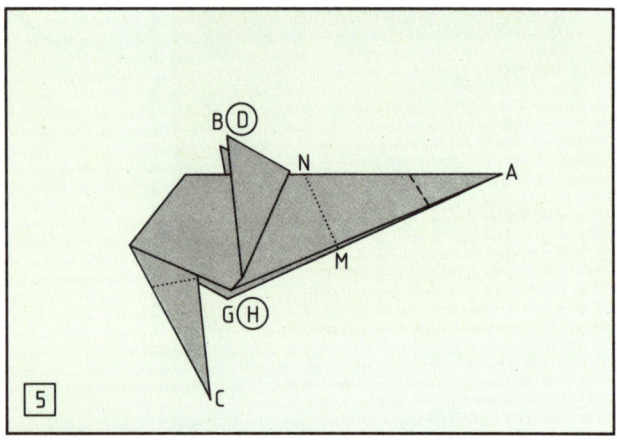

5. Inside reverse fold C again to form tail. Inside reverse fold A along dotted line, then outside reverse fold along dash line.

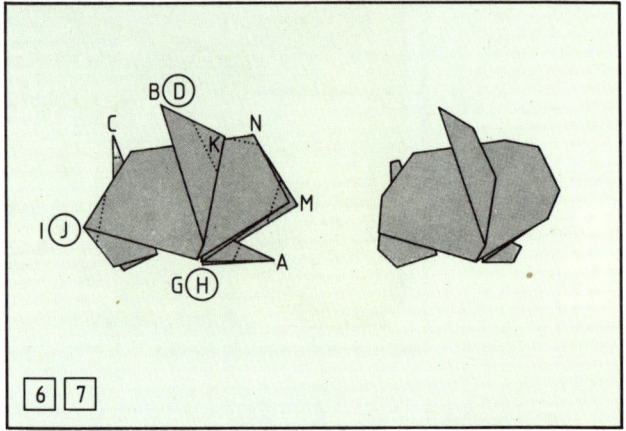

6. Inside reverse fold C to shorten tail. Inside reverse fold A along dotted line. Fold I and J to the inside of model along dotted lines. Fold K to the inside in front and back of model. Fold M to the inside in front and back of model. Slightly push in N.
7. The finished model.

CRANE

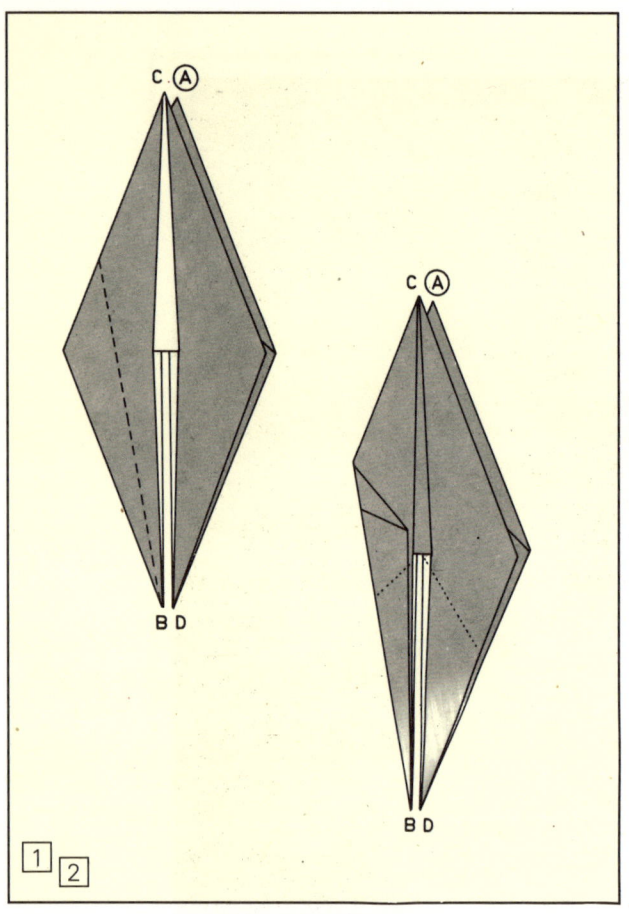

1. Start with Basic Form E. Valley fold B in front and back along dash line.
2. Inside reverse fold B and D.

3. Fold along lines 1 and 2 to form neck and head. Valley fold D in front and back.

4. Fold B in, then out, to form beak. On right side of work, mountain fold along dotted line. Pull A forward and crease again to lie flat. Bend D up slightly. Bend wings C and A to outside.

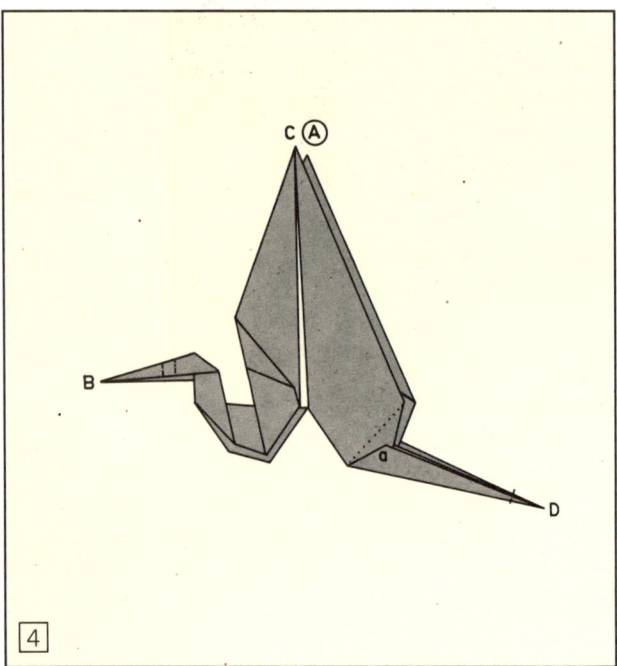

MONKEY

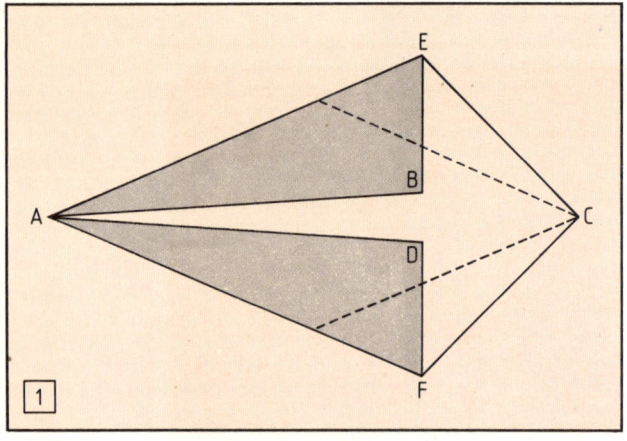

1. Start with Basic Form A. Valley fold C along dash lines.

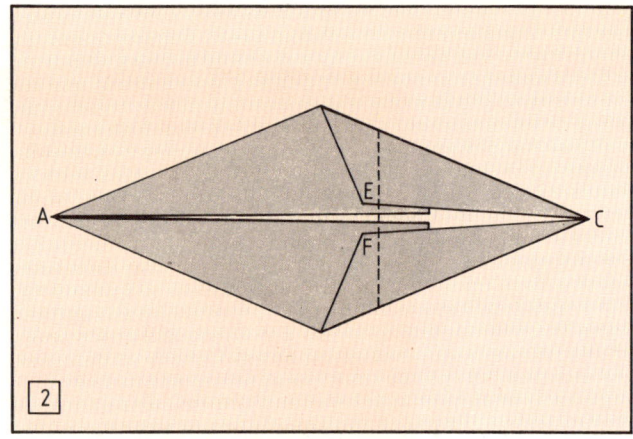

2. Valley fold C along dash line.

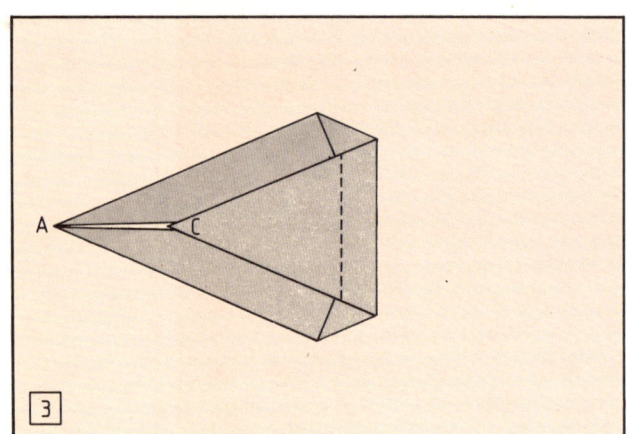

3. Valley fold along dash line, folding C to the right.

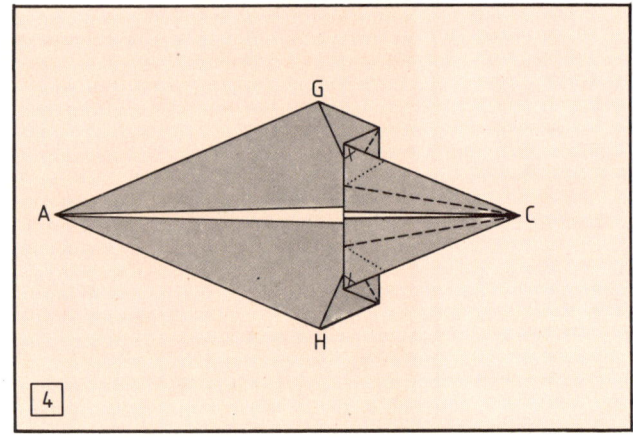

4. Valley fold along dash lines and mountain fold along dotted lines, pushing points x to position shown in diagram 5.

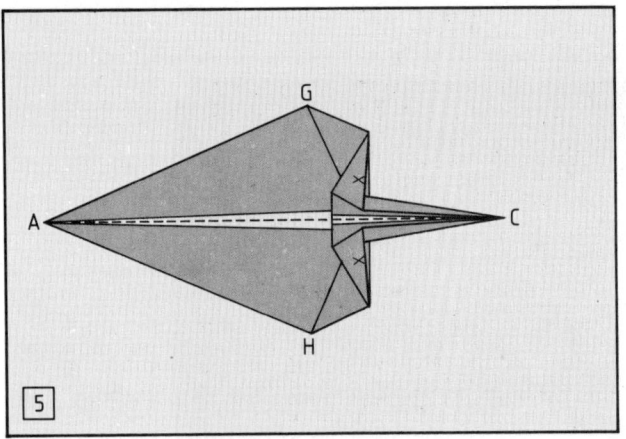

5. Valley fold along middle crease.

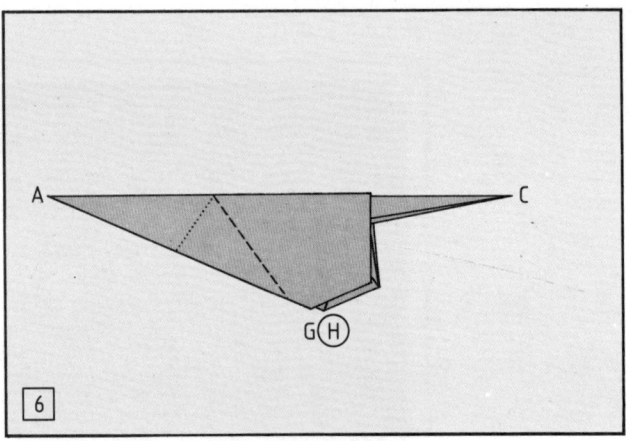

6. Valley fold A along dash line. Open up A and fold down in front to shape head as in diagram 7. Crease well.

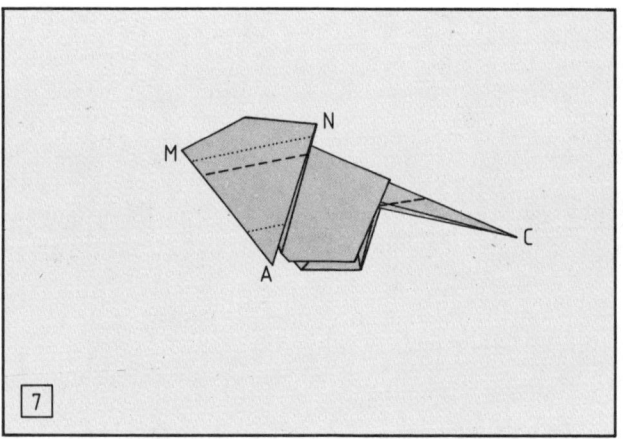

7. Mountain fold A along dotted line and valley fold along dash line to form head as in diagram. Outside reverse fold C.

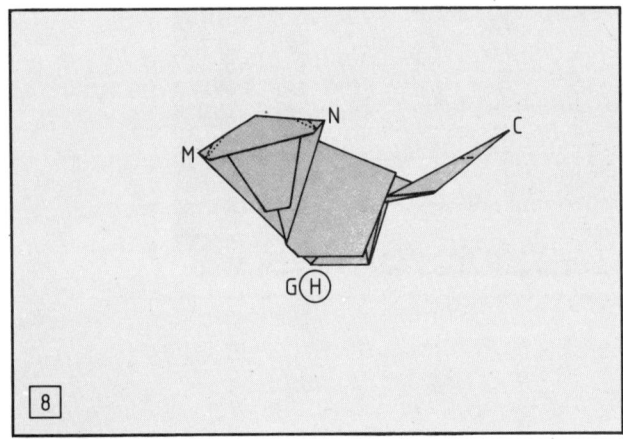

8. Fold M and N in, then out, to form ears. Outside reverse fold C.

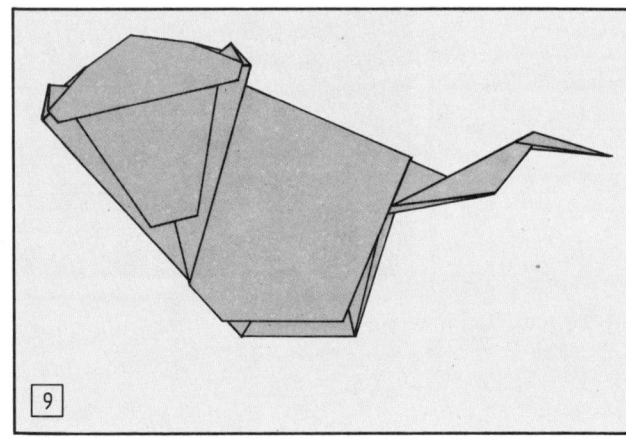

9. The enlarged, finished model.

WOLF

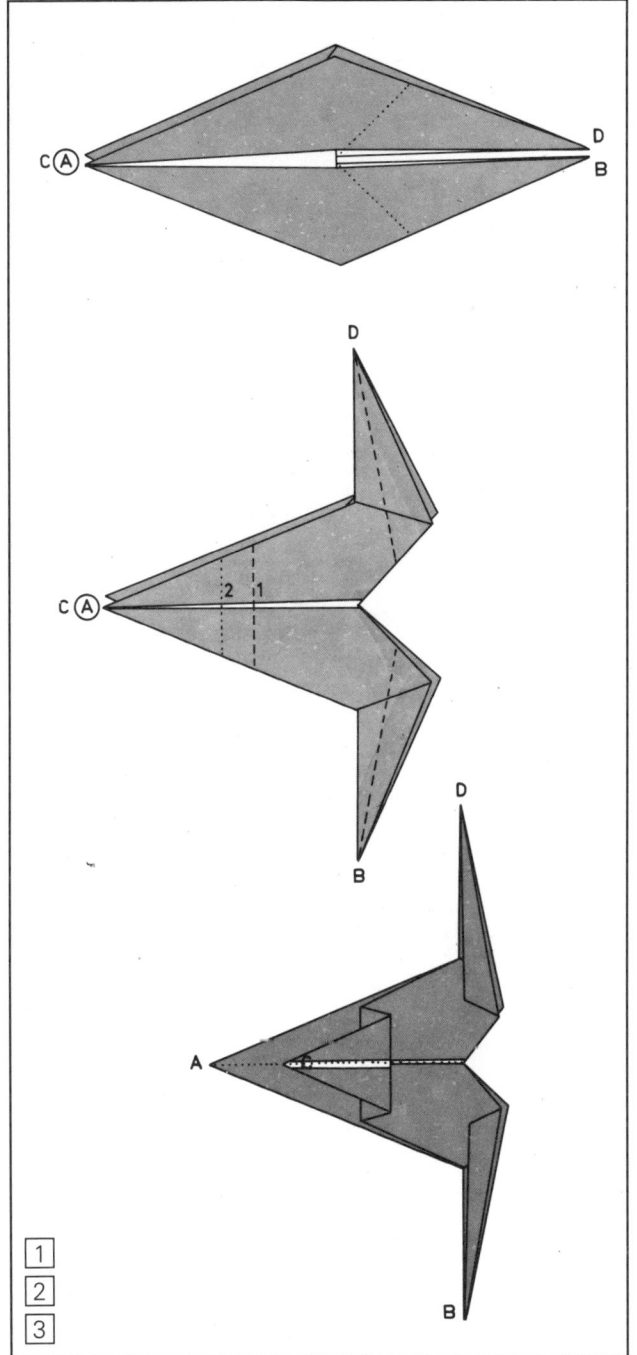

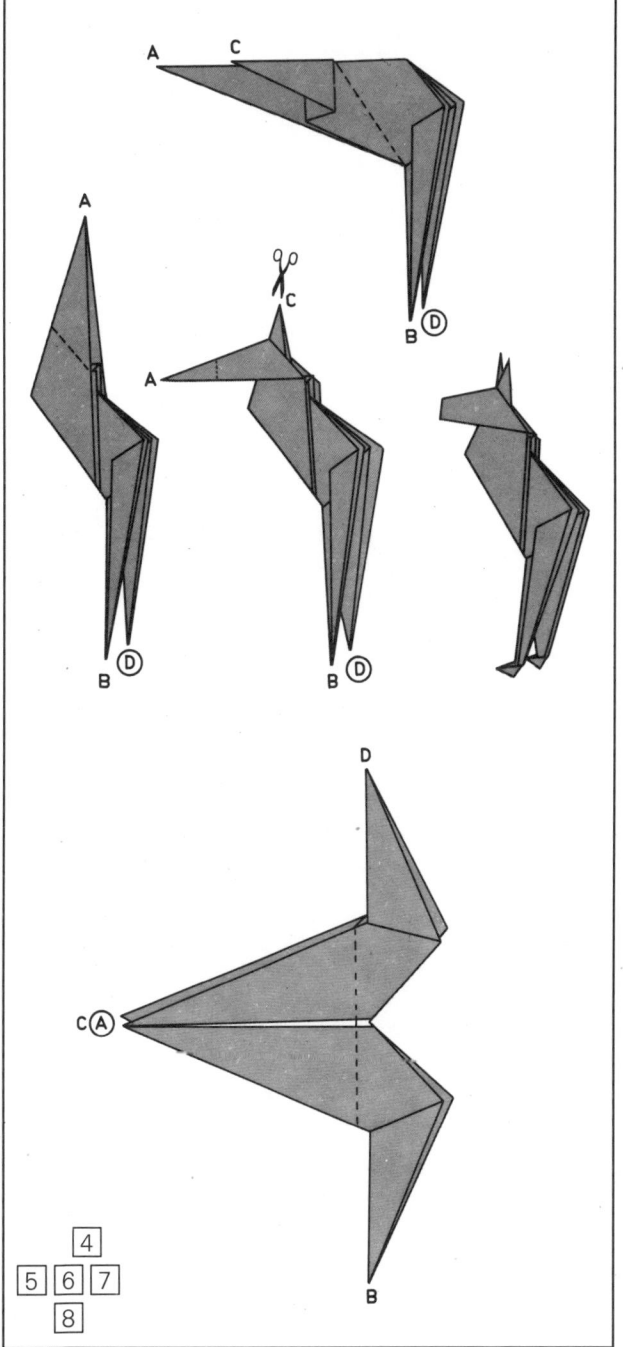

1. Start with Basic Form E. Inside reverse fold B and D.
2. Valley fold B and D in front and back. Valley fold C on line I and mountain fold on line 2.
3. Mountain fold along middle crease.

4. Outside reverse fold A and C along dash line.
5. Outside reverse fold A along dash line.
6. Cut C on fold line. Outside reverse fold B and D to make feet. Mountain fold A along dotted line.
7. The head and front legs are now done.
8. Using a second sheet of paper, prepare step 1 of front part of wolf. Fold C along dash line to the right.

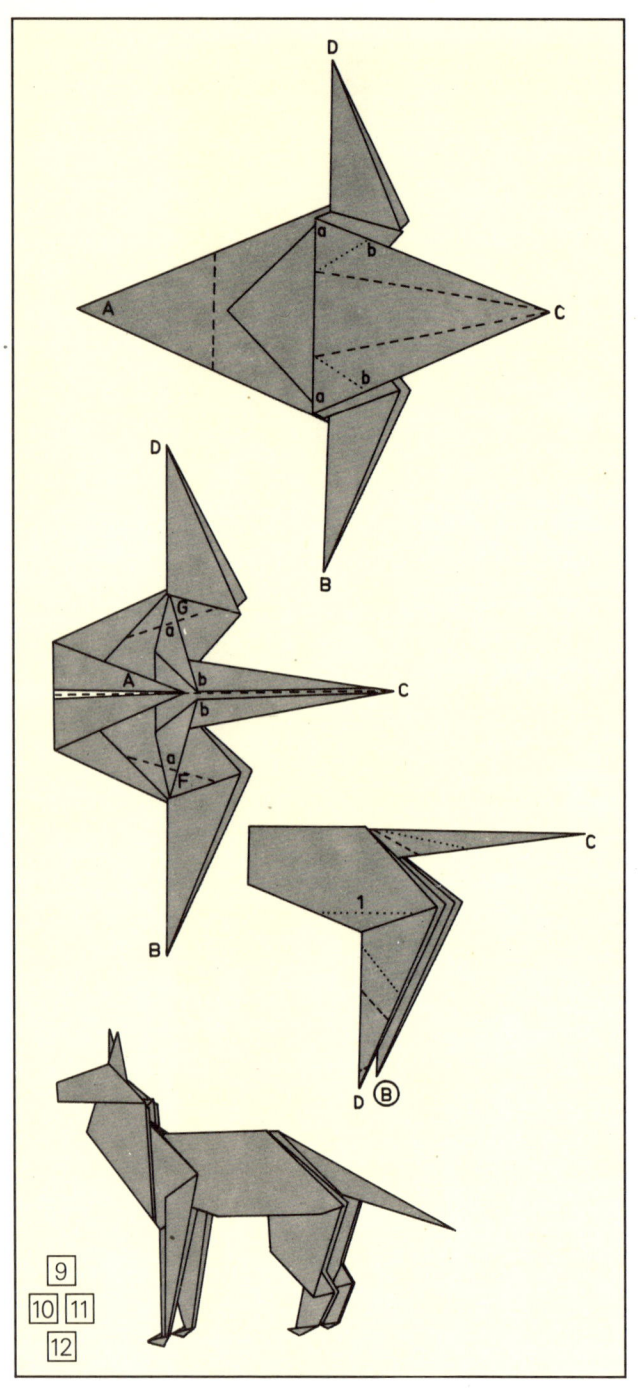

9. Valley fold C along dash lines. Mountain fold along dotted lines, pushing points a out to the right. Valley fold A along dash line.

10. Valley fold F and G along dash lines. Valley fold along middle crease.

11. Mountain fold in front and back along dotted line 1. To form tail and legs, inside reverse fold B, C, and D along dotted lines, then outside reverse fold along dash lines. Outside reverse fold to form feet.

12. Glue tail and head parts together.

OWL

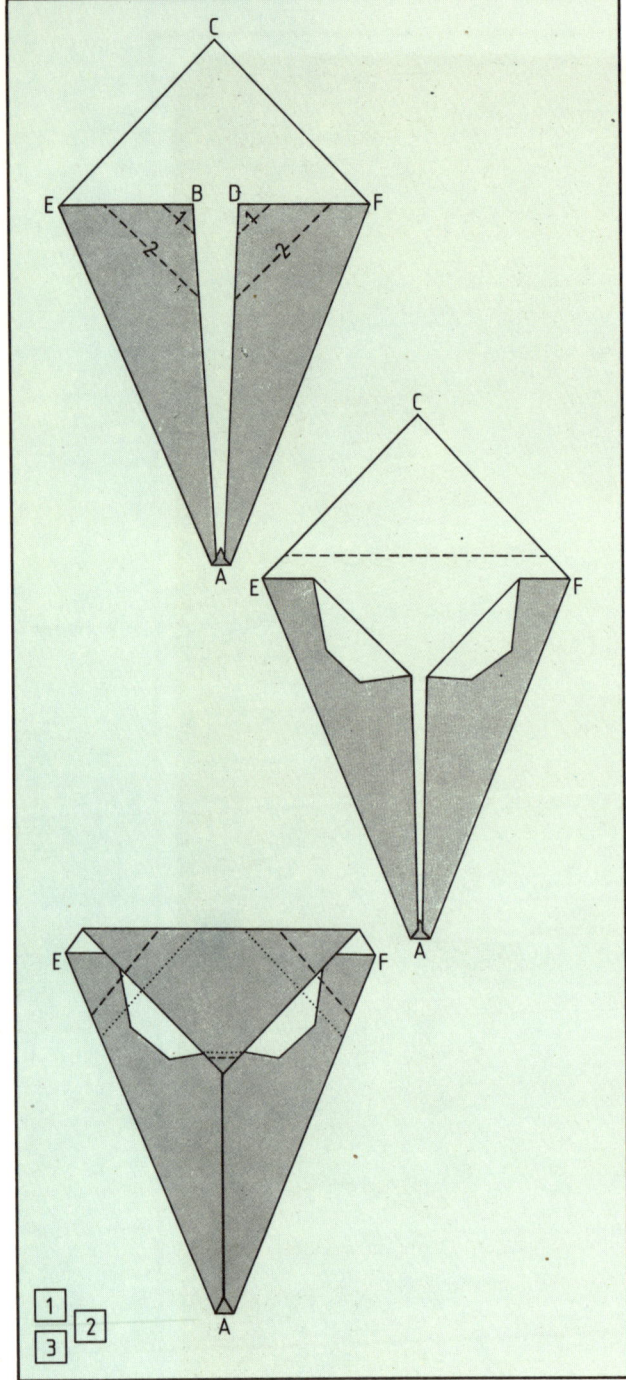

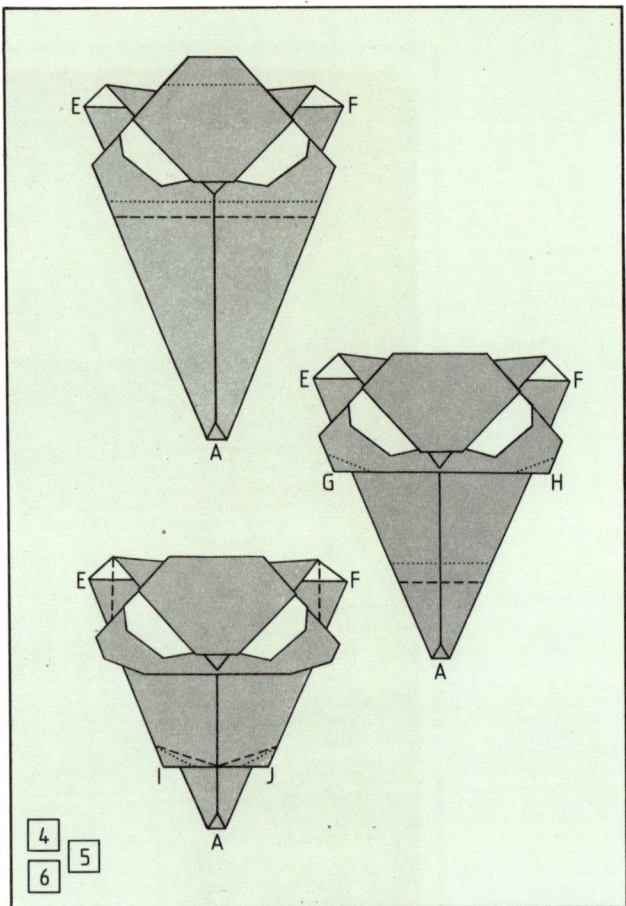

4. Mountain fold along dotted line. Mountain and valley fold underneath beak along dotted and dash lines to form head.
5. Mountain fold G and H. Mountain fold, then valley fold A to form tail.
6. Mountain fold, then valley fold I and J to form feet. Fold E and F along dash lines.

1. Start with Basic Form A. Fold A over a little, as shown in diagram. Valley fold B and D along dash lines 1 and 2.
2. Valley fold C along dash line.
3. Mountain fold, then valley fold C to form beak. Mountain fold, then valley fold E and F to form ears.

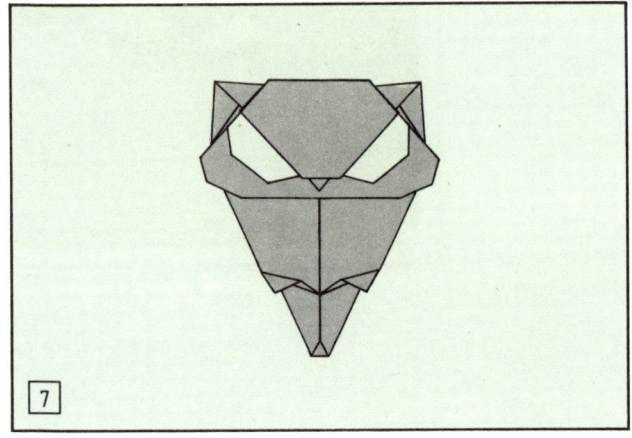

7. The finished owl.

TREE FOR OWL

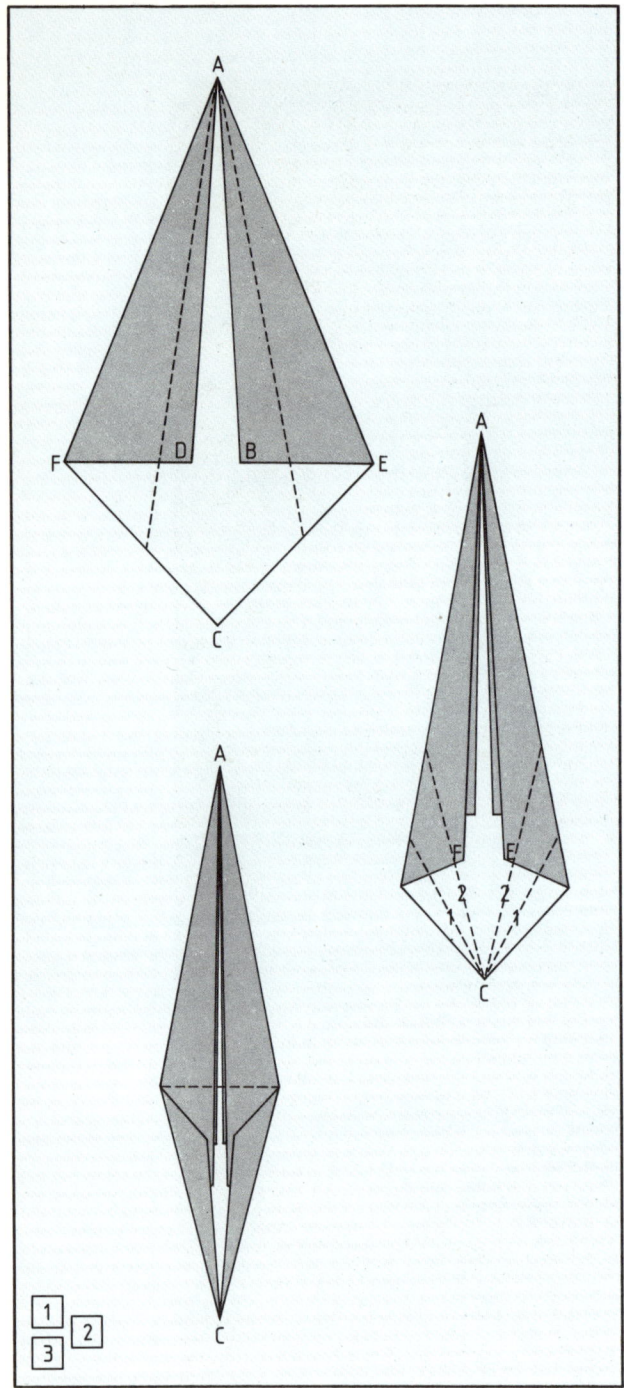

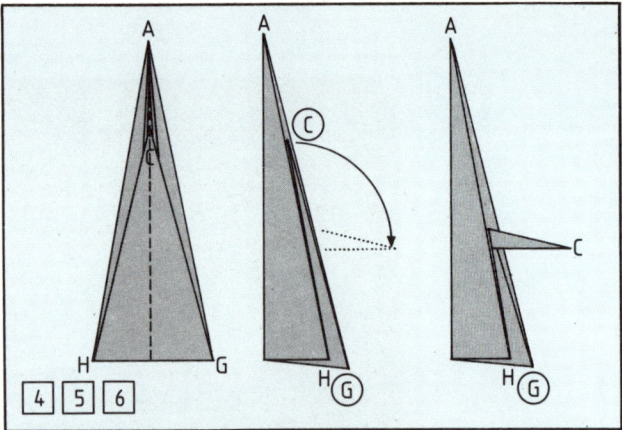

4. Valley fold along middle crease. C is now inside model.
5. Inside reverse fold C as shown.
6. The finished model.

1. Use a larger sheet of origami paper than was used for the owl. Start with Basic Form A. Valley fold A along dash lines.
2. Valley fold C along dash lines 1 and 2.
3. Fold C along dash line toward top of model.

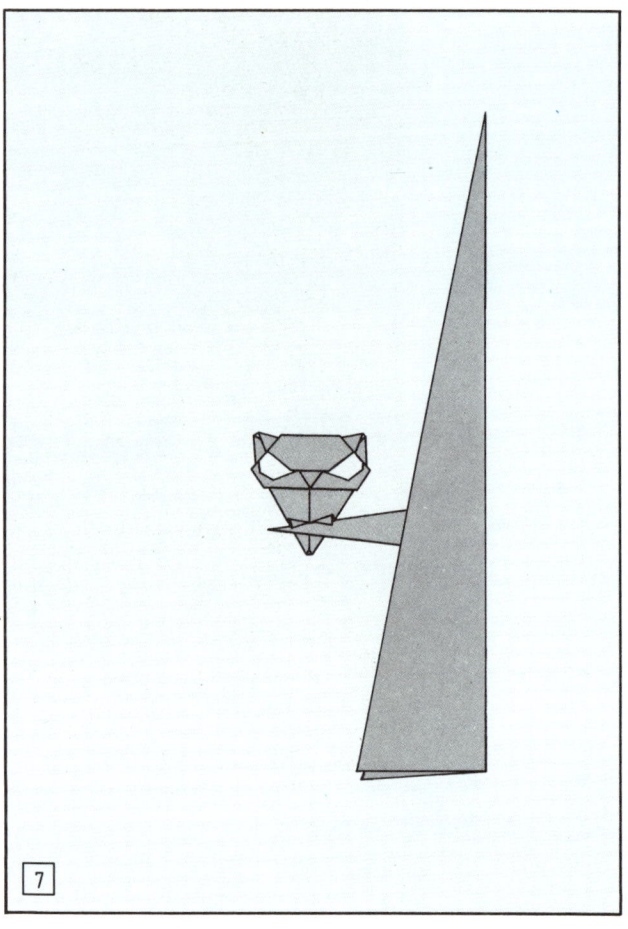

7. Glue the owl onto the tree.

OWL WITH WINGS

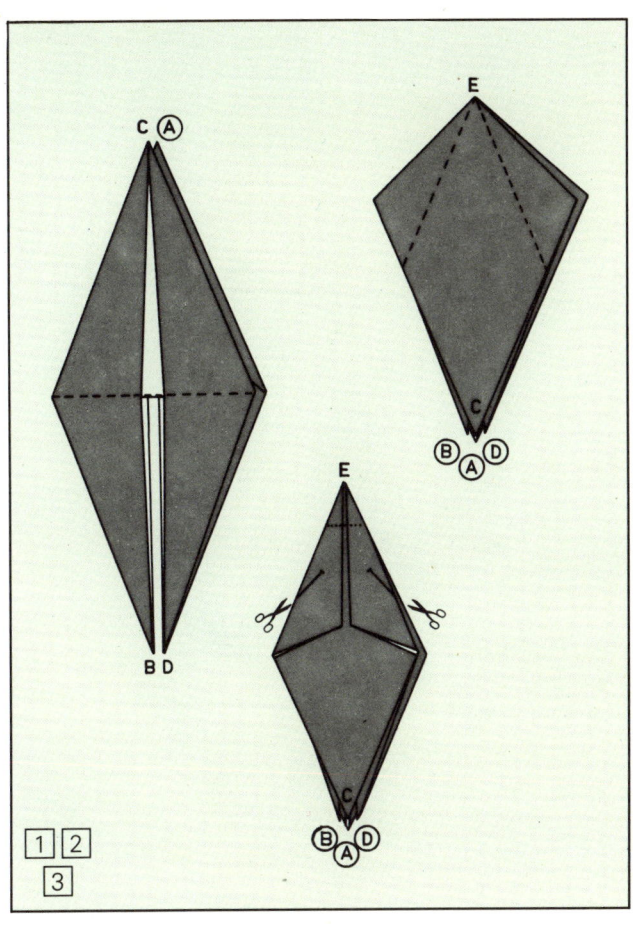

1. Start with Basic Form E. Valley fold C down along centre crease. Turn model over and fold A down along centre crease.

2. Valley fold in front and back along dash lines.

3. Mountain fold E. Cut top paper on shown lines and turn model over. Valley fold E along dash line.

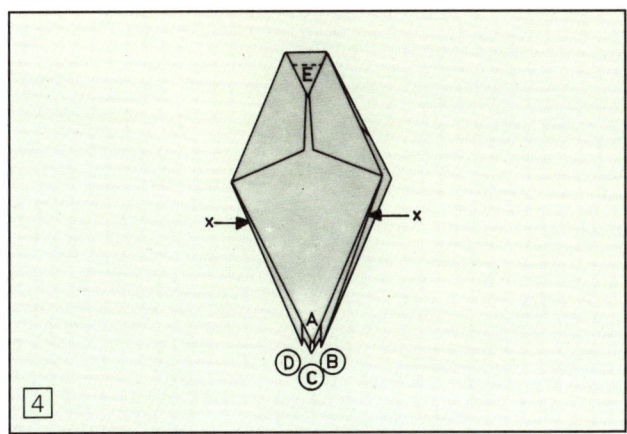

4. Pull B and D sideways, and push points x upward. Flatten wings and crease well.

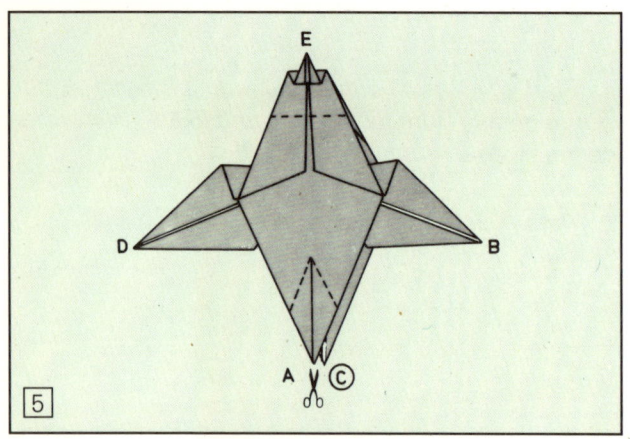

5. Valley fold E along dash line. Cut A and fold cut parts to the side along dash lines.

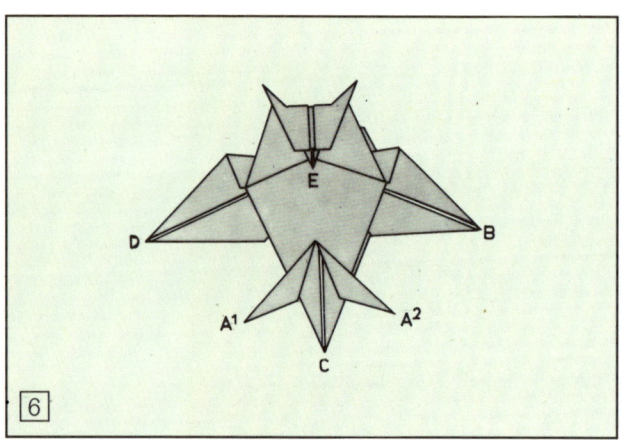

6. This is how your model should now look.

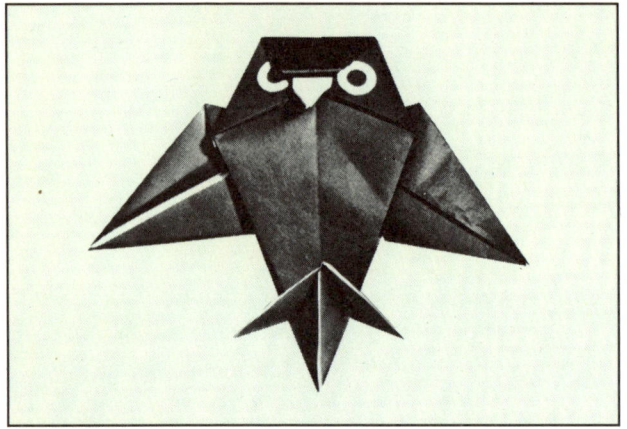

7. You may glue eyes on, if desired.

PEACOCK

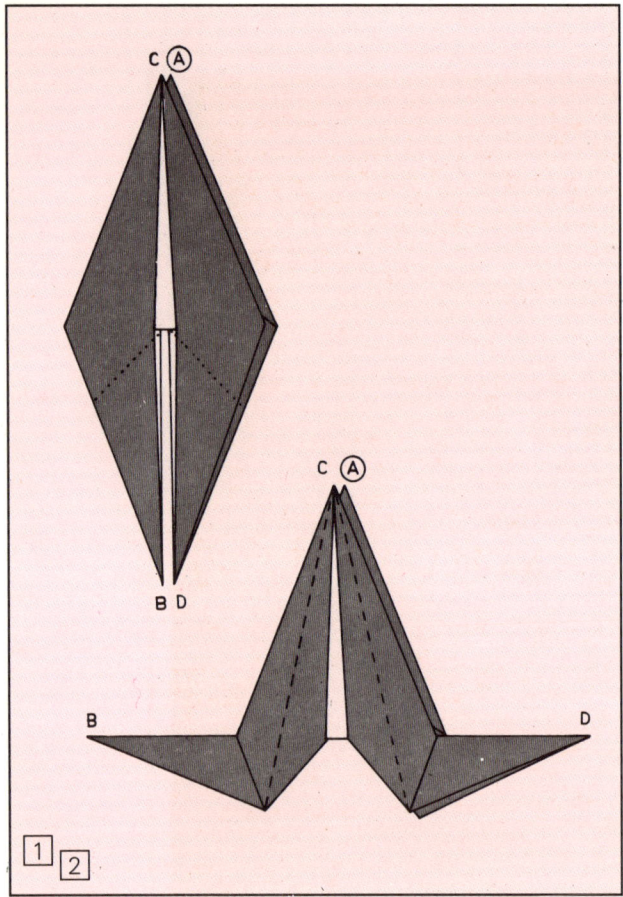

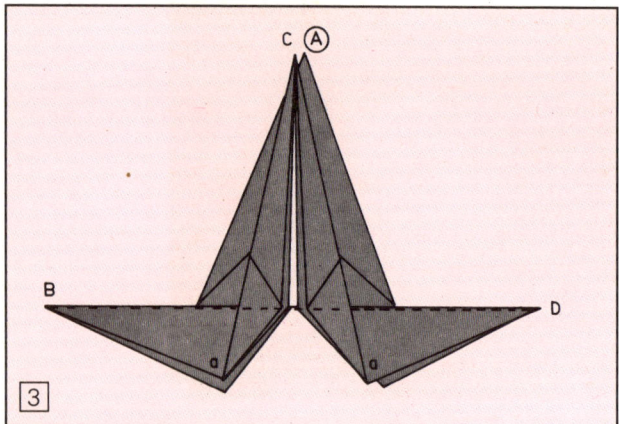

1. Start with Basic Form E. Inside reverse fold B and D.
2. Valley fold C.

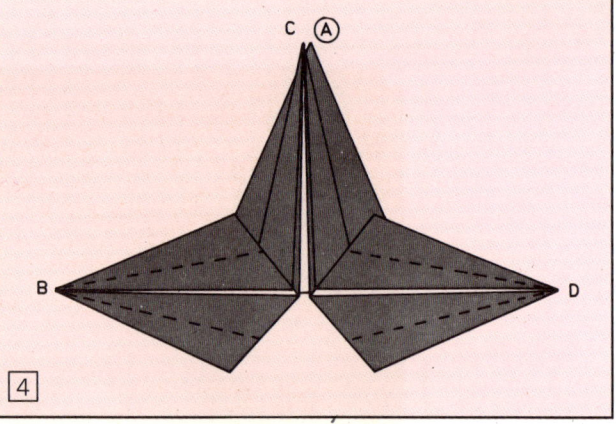

3. Fold A on left and right sides of model up into existing crease.

4. Valley fold B and D along dash lines. Pull A down in back so it is now on bottom of model.

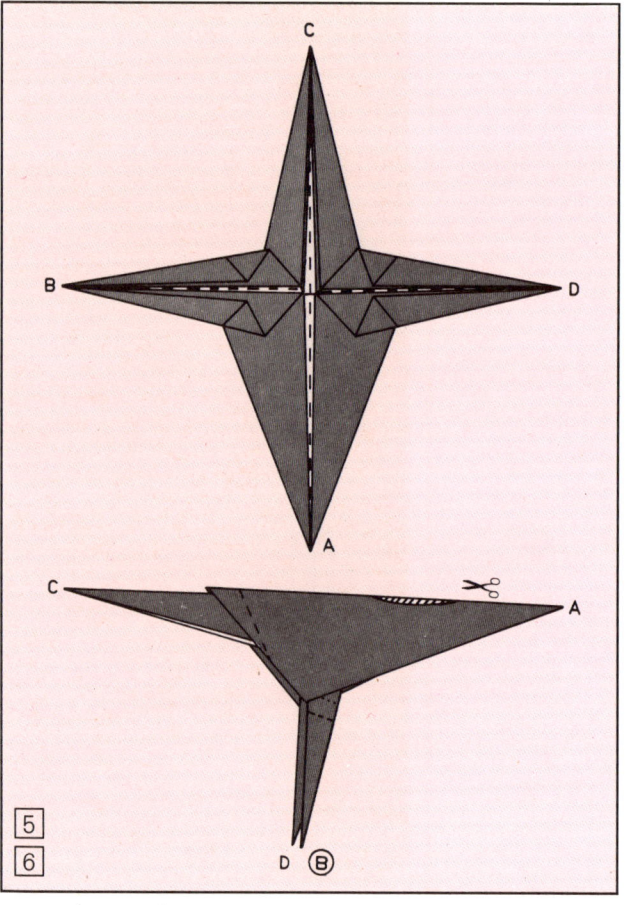

5. Valley fold B and D along existing crease. Valley fold along middle line and turn your work as in diagram.
6. Outside reverse fold C along dash line. Inside, then outside reverse fold B and D to form legs. Cut out as shown.

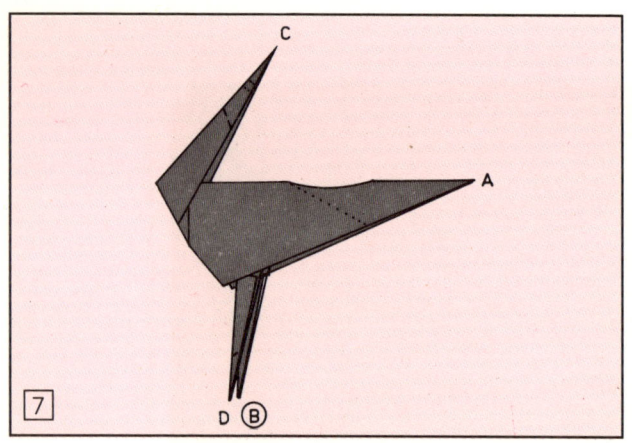

7. Inside and outside reverse fold C to form beak and head. Inside reverse fold A. Outside reverse fold B and D to form feet.

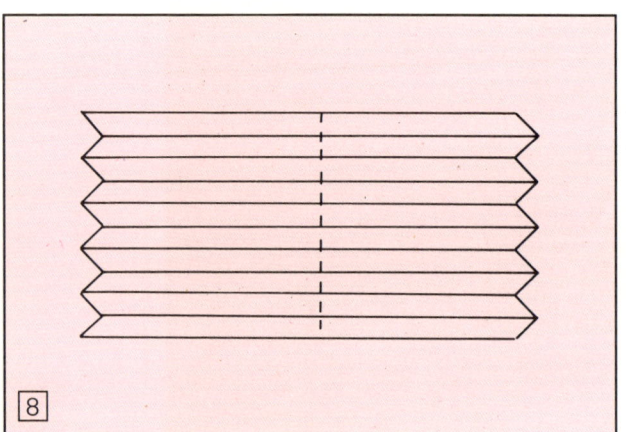

8. Fold piece of coloured paper like a fan.

9. Push folded paper in slit.

SAILBOAT

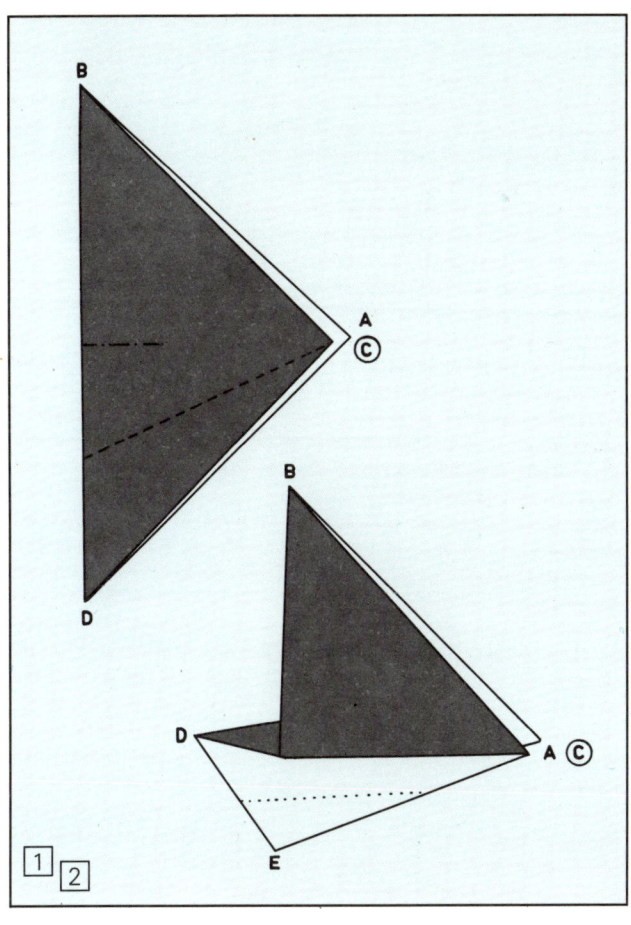

1. Place a square piece of origami paper with the coloured side facing down. Valley fold bringing tip A over to tip C.
2. Valley fold bringing D up to B. Unfold. Outside reverse fold along dash line, bringing D to the left. Mountain fold E along dotted line.

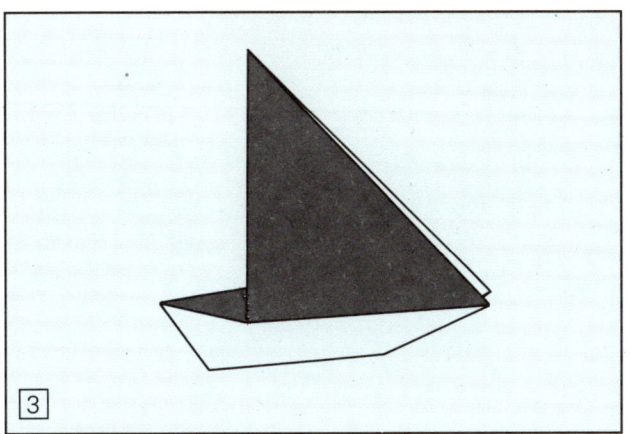

3. The finished sailboat.

FISH WINDSOCK

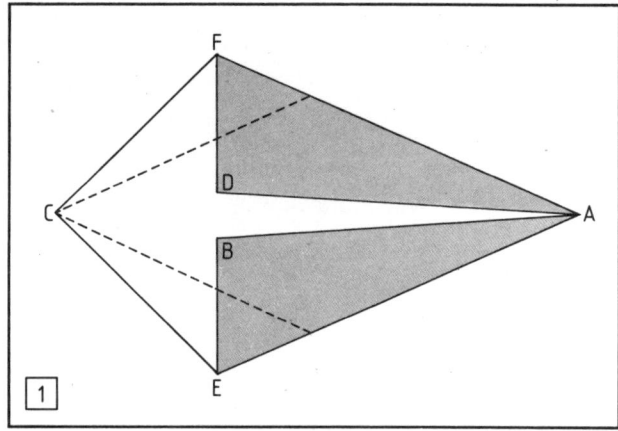

1. Use a piece of paper at least 25 x 25 inches. Start with Basic Fold A. Valley fold C along dash lines.

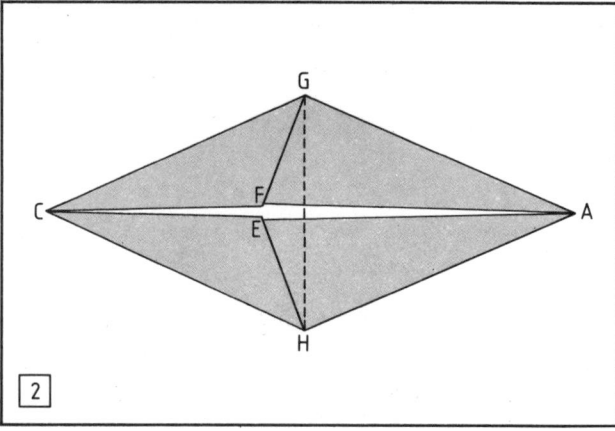

2. Valley fold along dash line, bringing C over to A.

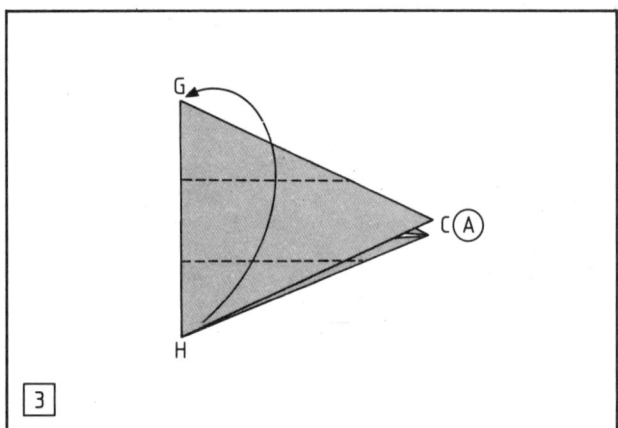

3. Valley fold H along dash lines. Valley fold G along dash line, over H.

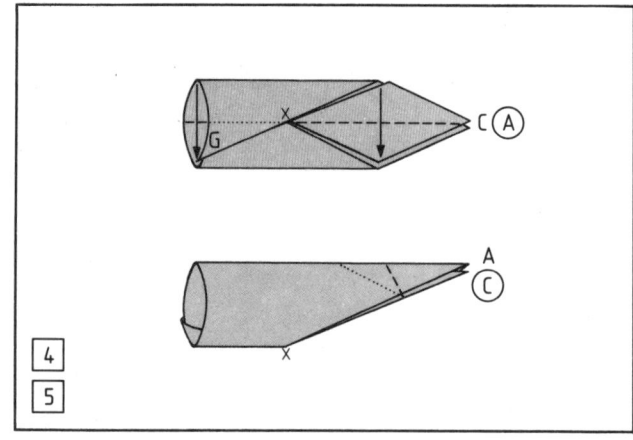
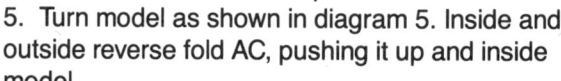

4. Roll model into tube shape.
5. Turn model as shown in diagram 5. Inside and outside reverse fold AC, pushing it up and inside model.

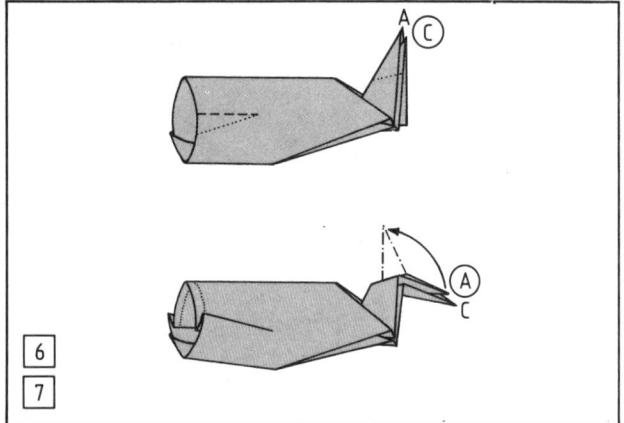

6. Inside reverse fold AC. Mountain and valley fold forward and back on round opening to form mouth.
7. Fold A and C sideways. Firmly crease mouth folds inside model.

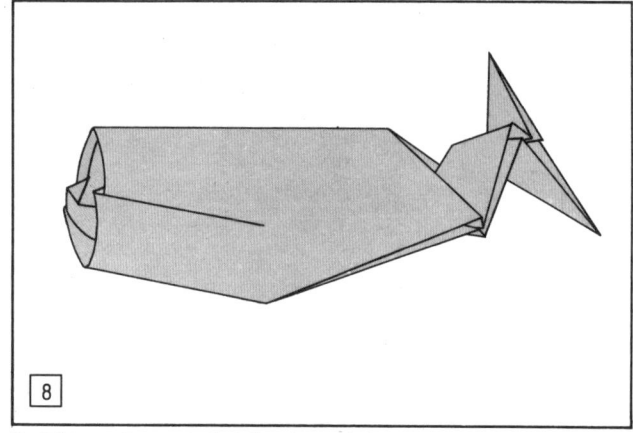

8. The enlarged, finished model.

PINWHEEL

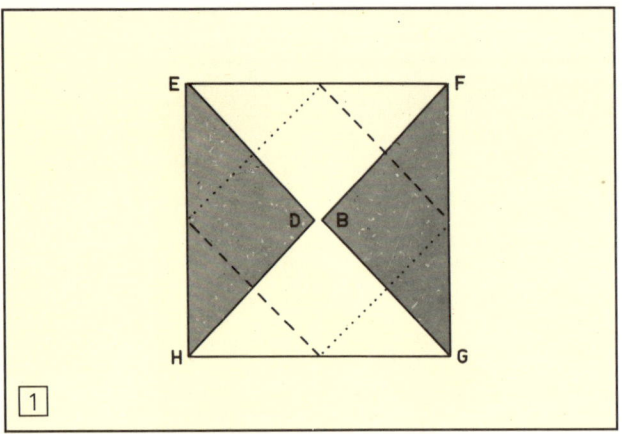

1. Start with Basic Form C, except A and C should be folded to middle point in back.

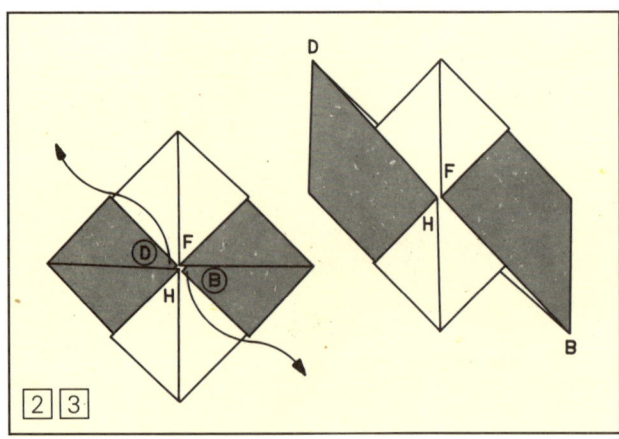

2. Valley fold corners F and H to the front and mountain fold corners E and G to the back onto middle point.

3. Hold the middle point with your thumb and pull out crease in middle of D. Refold as shown. Repeat with B. Turn model over.

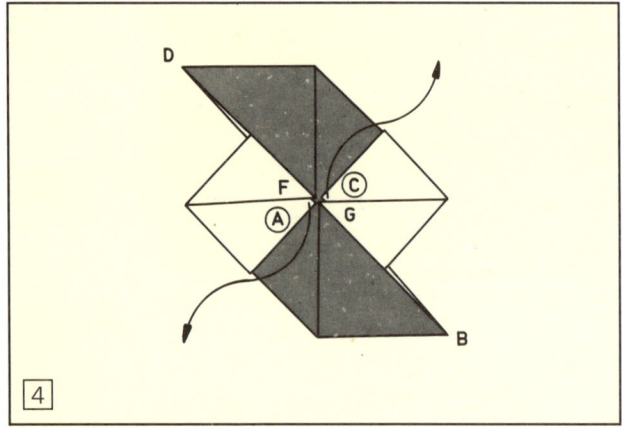

4. Pull out and fold A and C the same way as you did B and D.

ROSE

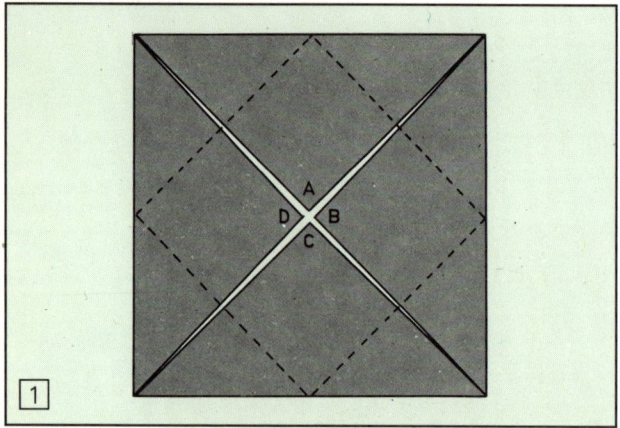

1. Start with Basic Form C. Fold all corners in to middle point.

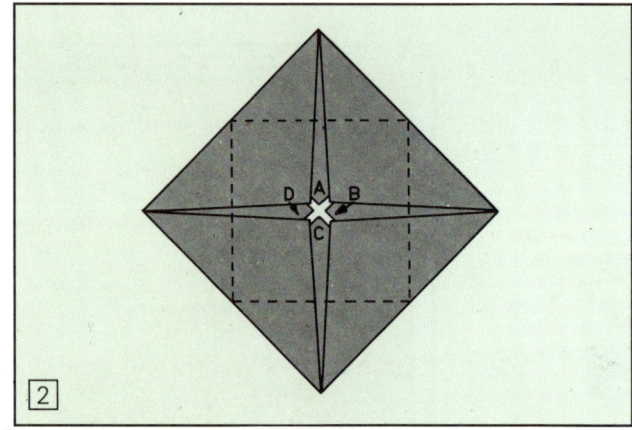

2. Fold all corners in to middle point again.

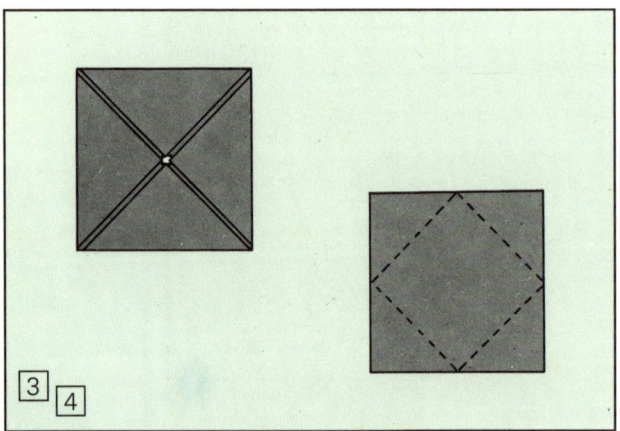
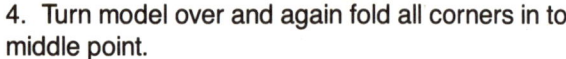

3. Your model should now look like this.
4. Turn model over and again fold all corners in to middle point.

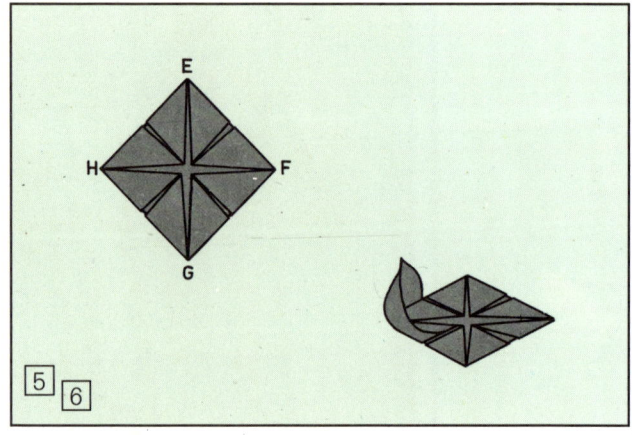

5, 6. Carefully pull up E, F, G, and H until they stand up.

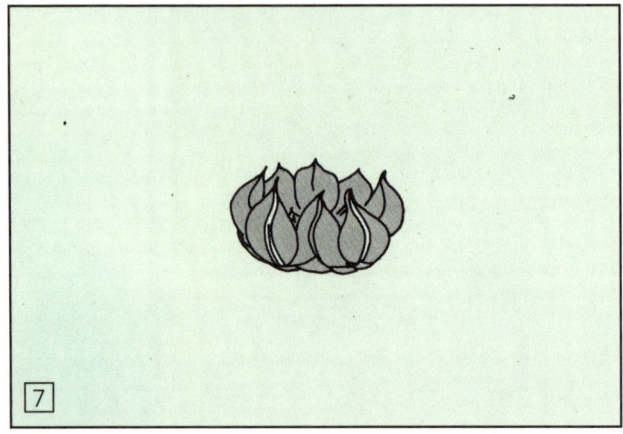

7. Pull the remaining corners in back gently to the front.

8. The rose makes a decorative cloth napkin.

STEM

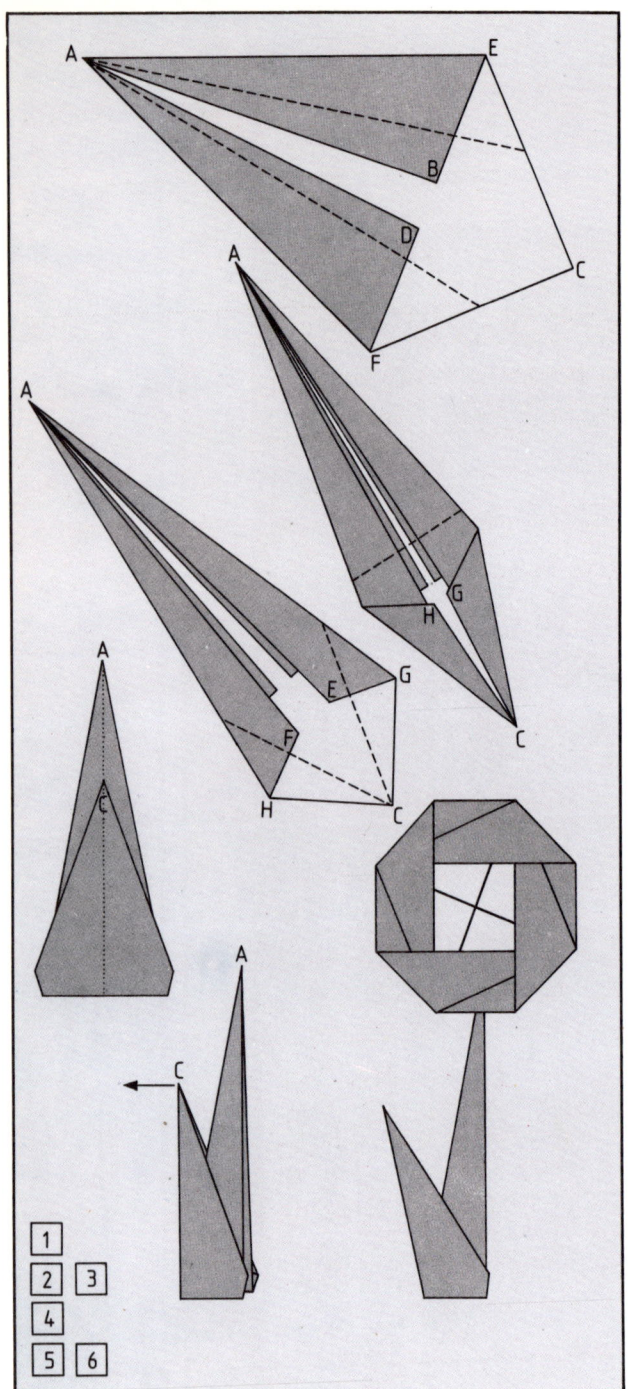

1. Start with Basic Form A. Valley fold along dash lines.

2. Valley fold along dash lines.

3. Fold C along dash line.

4. Mountain fold along middle crease.

5. Pull C sideways to form leaf. Crease bottom folds again firmly.
6. Glue Gentian Flowers or Lilies (see following models) on top of stem.

GENTIAN FLOWER I

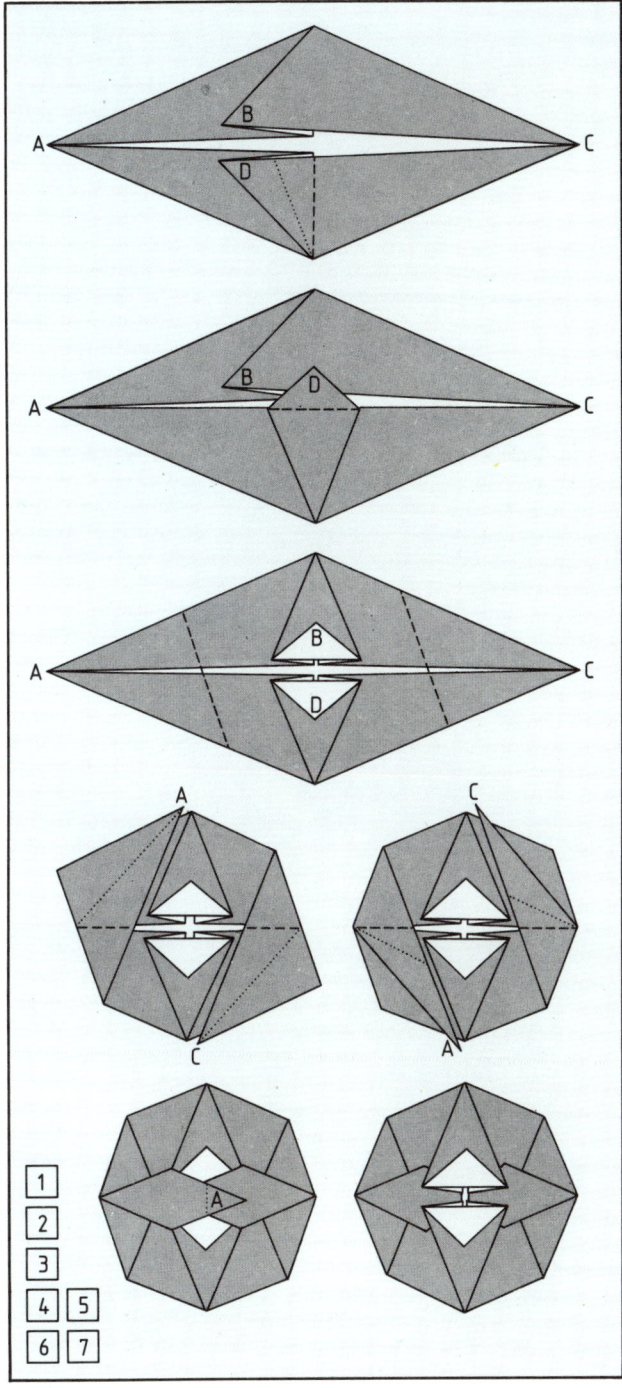

1. Prepare step 2 on page 26. Pull D until it is sticking up in the air, then push down along its centre crease until model resembles diagram.

2. Valley fold D. Fold B in the same way as D.

3. Valley fold along dash lines.

4. Using mountain and valley folds, bring A and C to position shown in diagram 5.
5. Using mountain and valley folds, bring A and C flat to middle of model.

6. Mountain fold A and C along dotted lines. Push A and C underneath B and D.
7. The finished flower.

GENTIAN FLOWER II

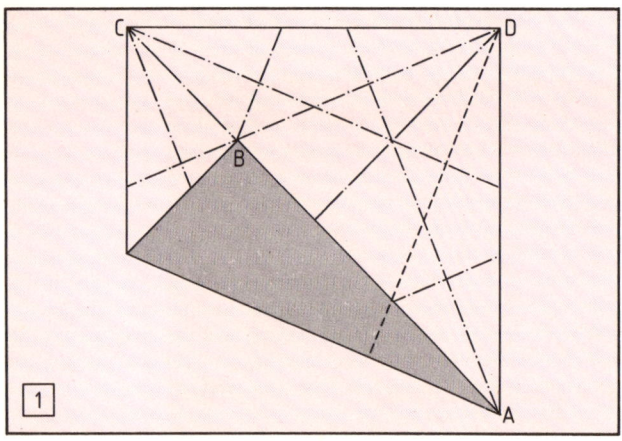

1. Start with Basic Form A. Unfold tip D and refold to form edge A-D, as shown in diagram 2.

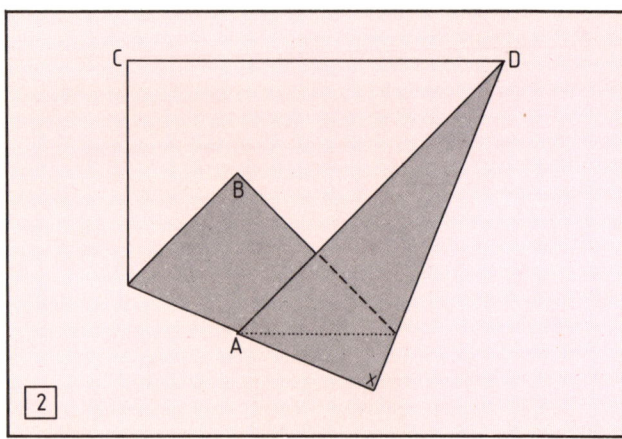

2. Valley fold on dash line and mountain fold on dotted line so A and x are positioned as in diagram 3.

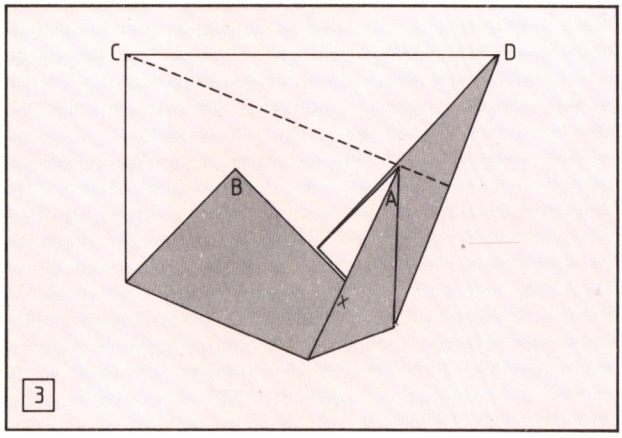

3. Fold C-D along centre crease.

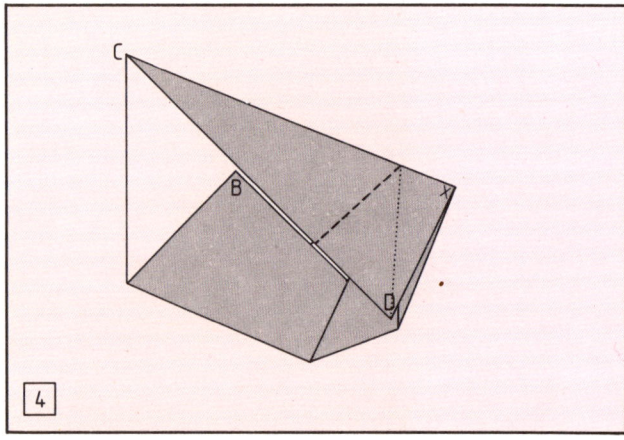

4. Valley fold along dash line and mountain fold along dotted line until x is positioned as in diagram 5.

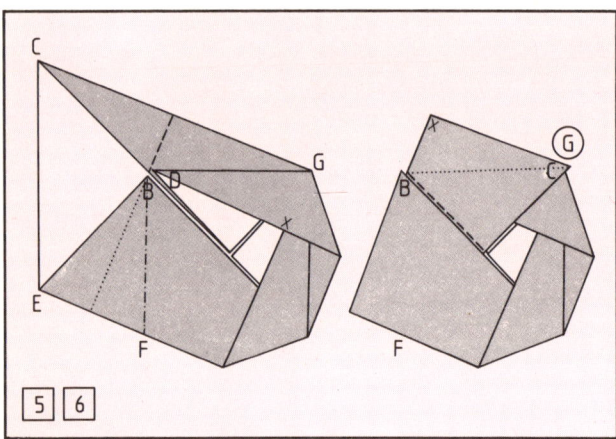

5. Along the dotted line, fold B-C under crease B-F.
6. Fold C on top of G. Valley fold along dash line and mountain fold along dotted line until x is positioned as in diagram 7.

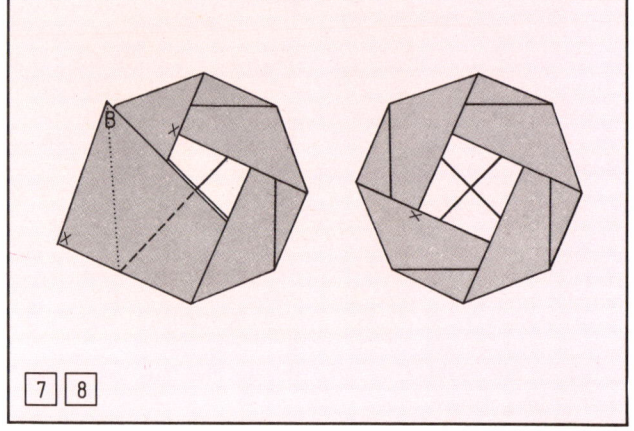

7. Valley fold along dash line and mountain fold along dotted line until x is positioned as in diagram 8. B is placed under tip A.
8. The finished flower.

DAFFODIL

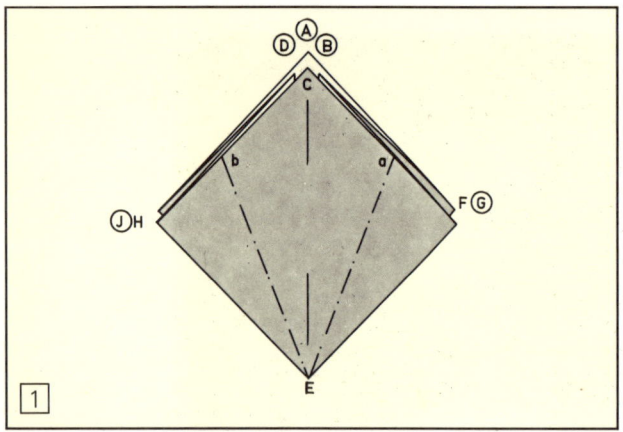

1. Start with Basic Form D. Crease along dash lines in front and back, Unfold.

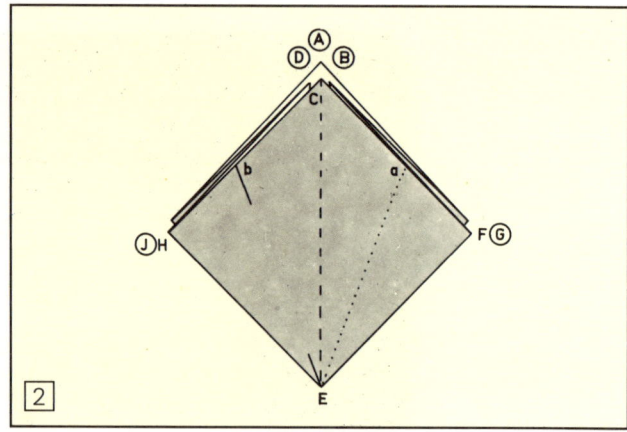

2. Using a mountain fold, pull points a and b so F is on centre crease.

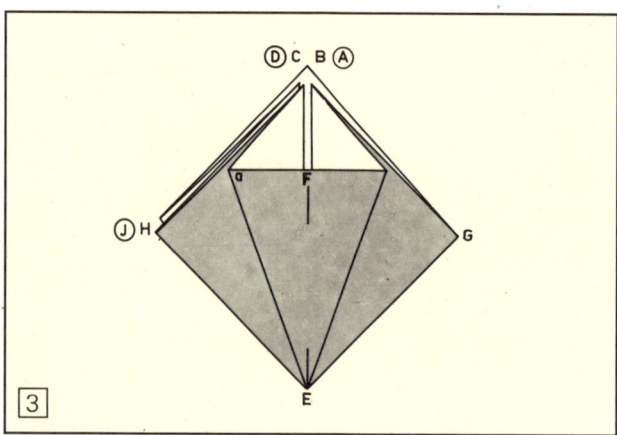

3. Repeat step 2 with corners G, H, and J.

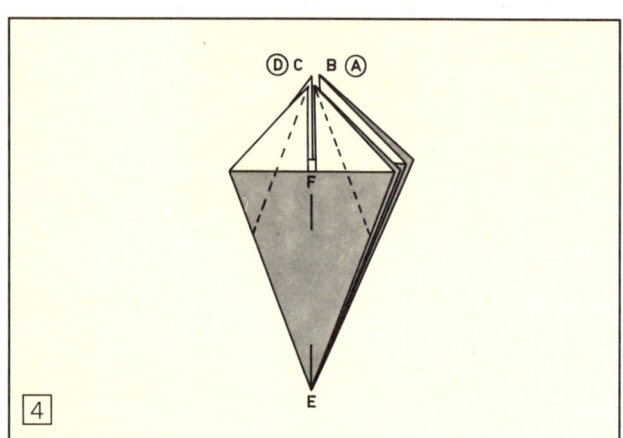

4. Valley fold on dash lines on all 4 sections.

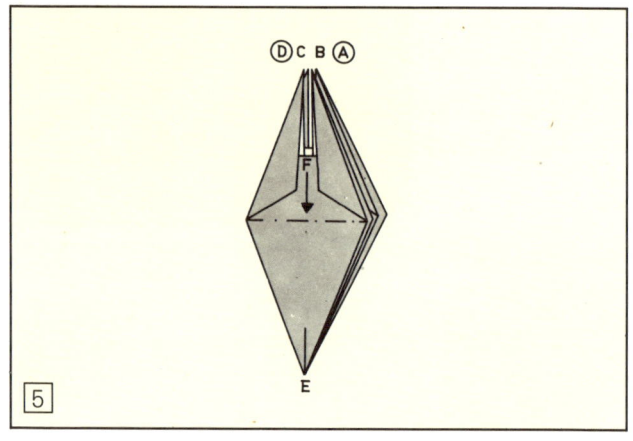

5. Fold E along dash line. Unfold and pull F down on existing crease. Repeat on all four sections.

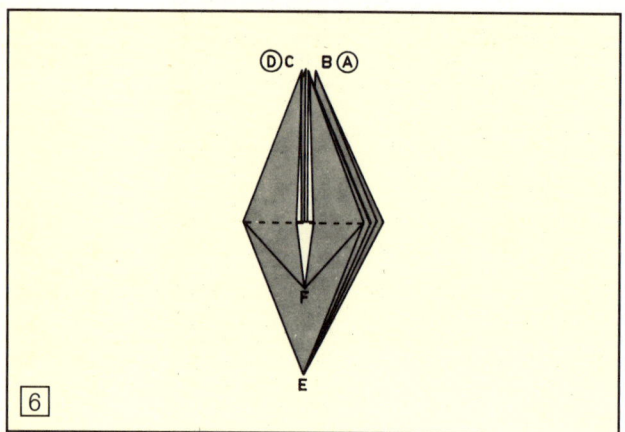

6. Fold up F. Repeat on all 4 sections.

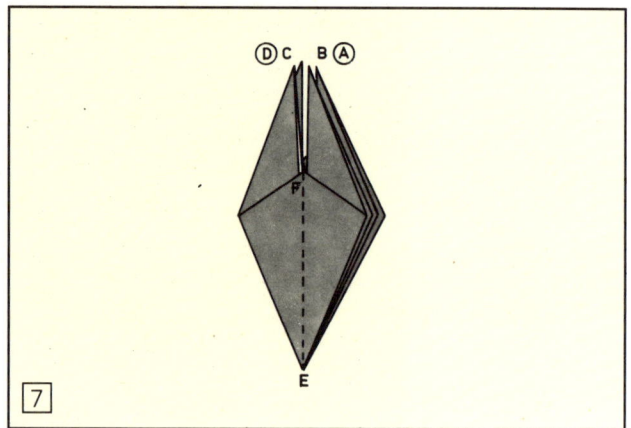

7. Fold C-E to the right along centre line.

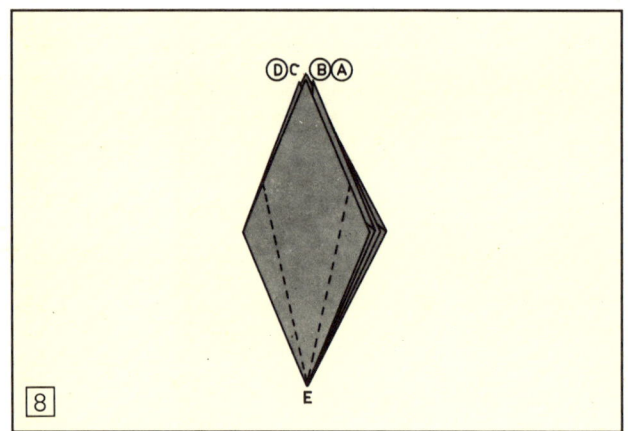

8. Valley fold along dash lines on all 4 sections.

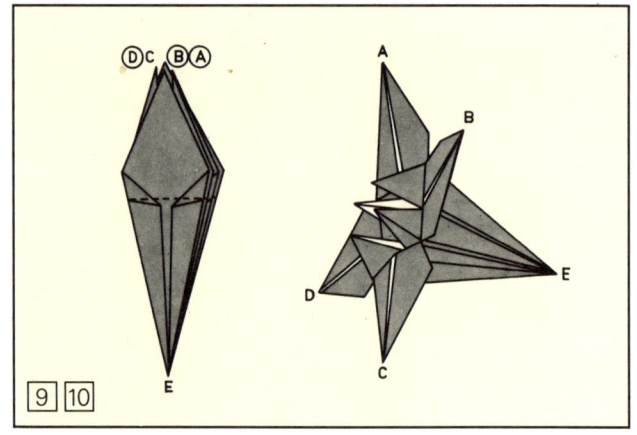

9. Fold flower petals outward.
10. The finished flower.

FLOWER STEM

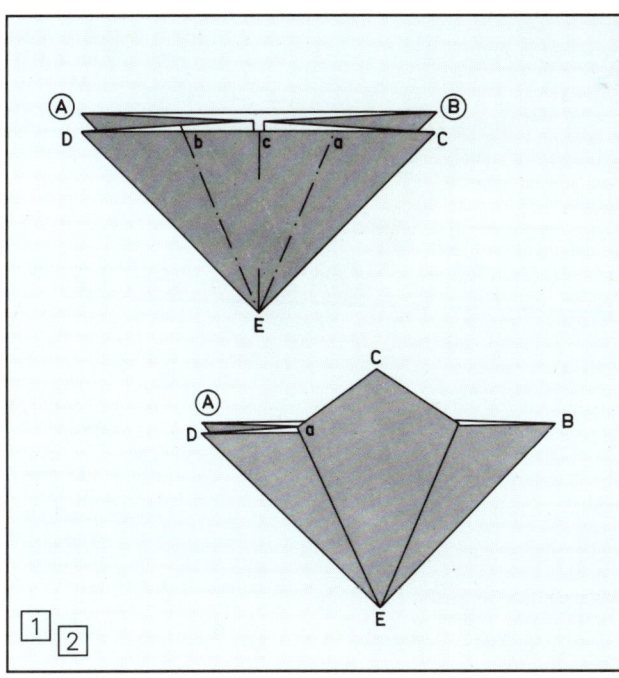

1. Start with Basic Form B. Crease along dash and dotted lines. Unfold. Pull C upward and, at the same time, crease line a onto line b.
2. Pull D, B, and A up and crease in the same manner as C. Fold each section behind C, on middle line.

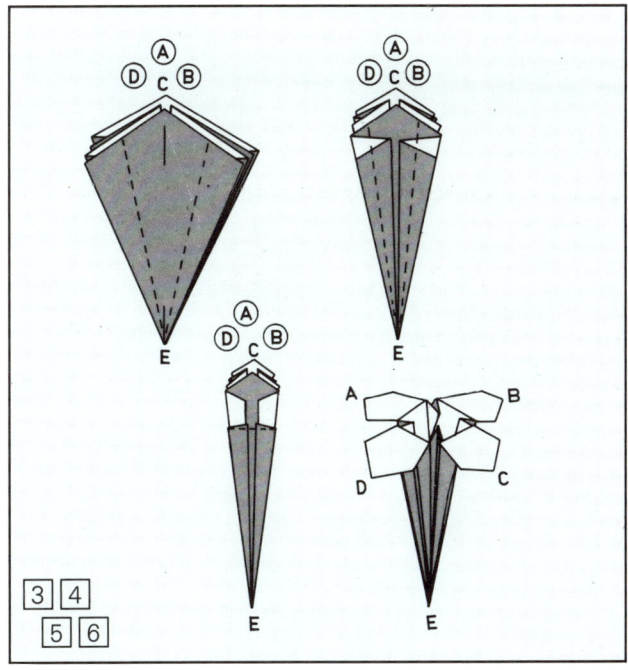

3. Valley fold along dash lines on all sections.
4. Valley fold along dash lines on all sections.
5. To open, fold A, B, C, and D to the outside.
6. This makes an attractive holder for the flowers.

BUTTERFLY

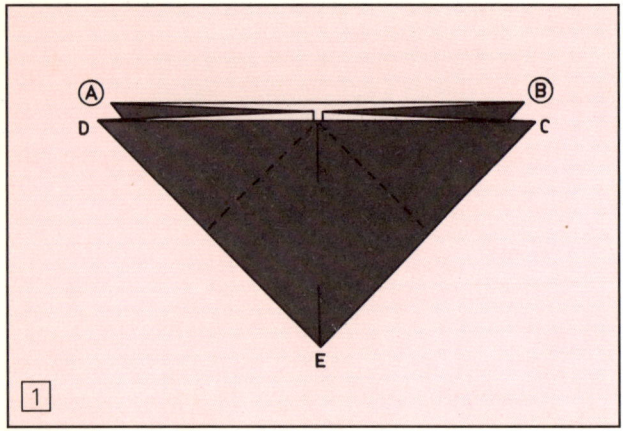

1. Start with Basic Form B. Valley fold C and D along dash lines.

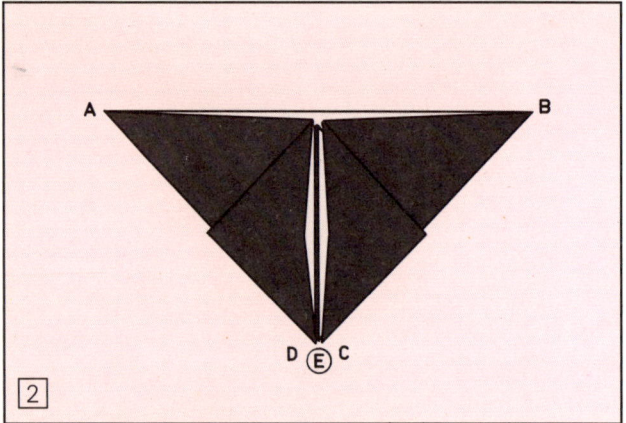

2. Turn model over as shown in diagram 3.

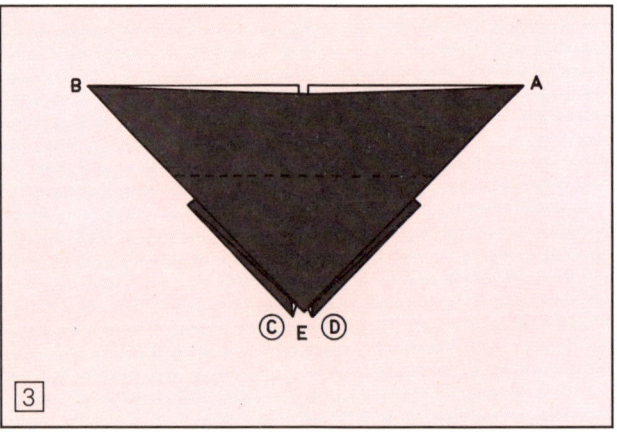

3. Valley fold C, D, and E along dash lines (see diagram 4).

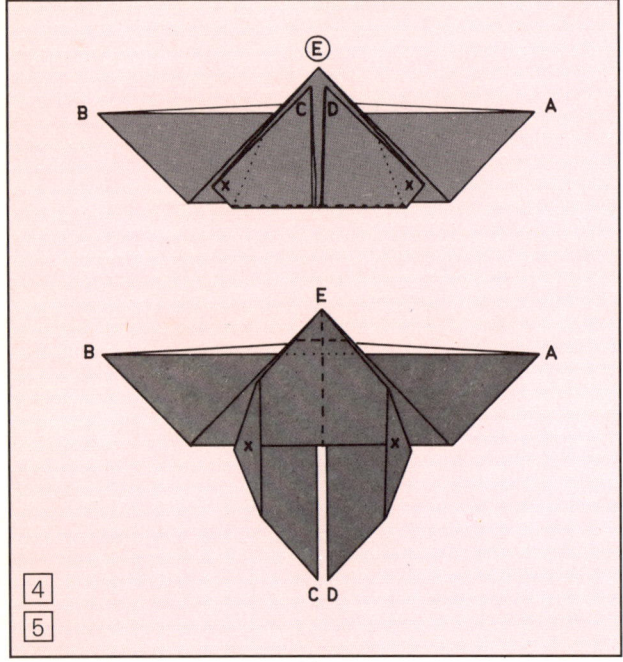

4. Fold down C and D, folding x in toward the middle.
5. Mountain and valley fold E. Valley fold along centre line.

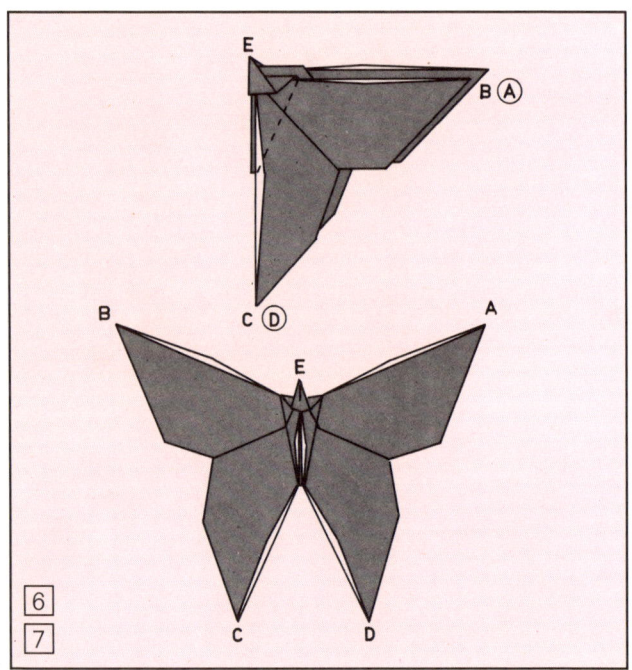

6. Valley fold along dash line in front and back.
7. The finished butterfly.